The Cultural Concept of Christianity

by

ARTHUR WALLACE CALHOUN

Dean, Sterling College,
Sterling, Kansas

AUTHOR OF

Social History of the American Family,
The Worker Looks at Government,
The Social Universe, etc.

2-56

WM. B. EERDMANS PUBLISHING COMPANY
Grand Rapids   1950   Michigan

THE CULTURAL CONCEPT OF CHRISTIANITY
by Arthur Wallace Calhoun

Set up and printed, August, 1950

To My Sons
DONALD AND ROBERT
In Recognition
of
Their Encouragement

PREFACE

The purpose of this book is to exhibit the meaning of Christianity as implicit in the modern view of life.

Because the conception of science and society herein presented is at odds with conceptions generally prevalent and deeply entrenched, considerable repetition has been deliberately introduced, but not more than is necessary for an intimate awareness of the nature of the psychological revolution necessary for the salvation of mankind. Even so, a reading of the book is but preliminary to the exacting thought and the unsparing action necessary in the present crisis.

Arthur Wallace Calhoun

Sterling College
June 1, 1950

CONTENTS

The Cultural Concept of Christianity

1

A WORLD TO WIN!

ALL thinking people are today in a state of confusion. Nature is not less reliable than of old, but man is about ready to admit that he cannot manage himself. Everybody above the level of the moron is neurotic, and nowhere in the world can we discover a wholesome social order. Man's difference from the animal has ceased to prove very helpful. People are more and more eager to go to school, but more and more uncertain as to what is worth learning. Most people are going on the assumption that we must keep busy, without any clear notion of whither our activity leads. The world is marking time and hoping against hope.

Perhaps under such conditions something is to be gained by sizing up human attainments so as to see whether there is any meaning in anything, whether there is anything really worthwhile, whether there is still some value in culture and personality. Certainly unless we can discover some grounds for the rallying of our energies in the direction of intelligence there will continue to be drift without mastery.

Now culture is social effectiveness. As an individual animal organism man would never have survived, let alone made any headway. As an animal herd he would have nothing to show for his existence. It can be argued, however, that the human race has made some progress; but whether that be true or not there are certain differences

1

from animal ways, and the fabric of those differences we call culture. We should like to think that the differences amount to something more than mere survival, though now we are beginning to wonder whether there is any assurance of even that.

But culture is social effectiveness, and if our culture is of doubtful value, as the present world predicament seems to indicate, we may well investigate the nature of our whole life-scheme in the hope of discovering wherein we come short. Perhaps, indeed, our biggest fault has been in taking man's ways for granted and assuming their general validity. Before we let the insects, or atomic radiations, take over, and supersede us, we may at least take stock of ourselves and see whether there is still hope of turning the scales in man's favor.

Because our age has been an age of science, the meaning of culture is for us expressed mostly in terms of science, though if politicians and militarists persist in telling scientists under what conditions they may operate, the resulting eclipse of science will usher in an age under necessity of expressing whatever culture is left in other than scientific terms. Meanwhile, however, students of our culture must first of all analyze the nature and meaning of science, which contains the germ of destruction, but possibly the germ of deliverance. At least our previous adventures in science have opened up vistas of glowing possibility, so that if there is a world to lose, there is, on the other hand, a world to win.

Mystical psychologists attribute to man a death wish, which in many individual instances results in suicide. Perhaps fewer people would take their own lives if they realized that such an act is merely a silly expression of an inflated ego: no human being is important enough to warrant such an episode! At present, however, the race seems to be yielding to a death wish. Man seems to be so intoxicated by achievement, so proud of his own puny importance, that he contemplates self-annihilation as an evidence. It may be, however, that he can still be challenged by the vision of a world to win.

At all events, such is the challenge of Christianity, whose prime reference is to the fortunes of this planet and its inhabitants; for in spite of all other-worldliness, Christianity is essentially rooted in this earth, and stakes its truth on the possibility of establishing on it the Kingdom of God and of making this kingdom dominant. Indeed the whole plot of the Bible is the evolution of this kingdom from initial germ to final mastery. It may be noted, also, that the perennial attraction of utopias points in the same direction. In spite of all preoccupation with petty, narrow, short-sighted aims, we are continually called back to the vision of a redeemed earth rising above the ruins of institutions and systems that have collapsed because devoted to exploitation and waste. It may well be that the big task of our generation is to merge all utopian hopes of a cooperative commonwealth in the spiritually envisaged Kingdom of God. Perhaps, indeed, if we once learn to think straight we can arrive.

2

MECHANISTIC THINKING

WHEN we reach for an intellectual solution to the human problem, we discover that because our modes of thought mirror our major experiences modern science has been thrown off the track by man's skill at invention; for ever since man became an undoubted success at piecing things together into workable contraptions he has been obsessed with his skill as inventor, and has so plumed himself on his own mastery that he has regarded the machine as the pattern of validity and has tried to interpret everything by analogy with the machine, so that his thinking has been mechanistic. To the sophisticated modern man, everything is a machine and every relation is mechanical. The very nexus of cause and effect is presumed to be identical with mechanistic gearing.

On this basis the universe is a machine, and if God exists he is a master-mechanic, a supernal watch-maker — whose clock is now running down. The animal body is a machine; man is also a machine, chiefly a composite of stimulus-response circuits. The mind is a machine — a summation of lifeless "elements" of sensation and feeling (which of course have no actual existence of their own, but are merely dead fragments dissected out by the skill of the psychologist so that the splinters can be thrown together again into the fiction of a personality). Society is likewise a machine composed of smaller machines, so

4

that we speak of "the machinery of government" as well as of "machine politics."

This is all very natural, for the only way we can understand anything is as a projection of our own experience. When we exert muscular energy, we have a feeling in our muscles that we identify with "force," and straightway "force" becomes a concept for understanding what happens when gravity operates or when electricity functions. Likewise when we get results by putting together a machine, we project our own experience into the work of creation and imagine God as making machines. As already remarked, many people have even come to think that expression of belief in causation amounts to the assertion that the relation is mechanical.

So matter-of-course is this mechanistic conception of reality that we scarcely realize that we are governed by it and that it shapes and controls our thinking and our doing. From top to bottom of our culture, everything is refracted by this stereotyped pattern, so that our whole scheme of existence is conditioned by this transitory makeshift. Consequently we are superficial and temporary in everything we think and say and do. Indeed our whole education is so possessed by the fleeting mechanistic illusion that the first step in intellectual and cultural emancipation must be the systematic eradication of the whole atmosphere in which we live and move and have our being. We must learn to see reality as organismic, integral.

Now a machine is an assemblage of parts according to an external pattern and for a purpose outside the machine itself. Moreover these parts are interchangeable and replaceable. To understand the machine, one takes it apart, reduces it into its ultimate elements, and examines their interworking. The mechanistic viewpoint, in fact, is that meaning resides in the parts of anything and is to be reached by dissection. When the ultimate fragments have been analyzed out, nothing more is to be said. The whole is thought to be equal to the sum of its parts and to require no other explanation.

According to this mechanistic interpretation, life is fragmentary and piecemeal. A man is eighty-nine cents' worth of chemicals, or thirty dollars' worth, or a few million dollars' worth, according to whether we are figuring in pre-inflation, or post-war, or post-atomic terms. The human body if thought of in the large is a creaky, bungled mechanism unworthy of any self-respecting craftsman! A good mechanic would have given us a microtelescopic eye, and immunity from structural defects such as induce sacro-iliac trouble, appendicitis, and hernia!

Medical practice reflecting such a mechanical, piecemeal view becomes mere quackery, a treatment of particulars, very likely a suppression of symptoms. It resorts nonchalantly to specific medication and surgery, and neglects to envisage the organism as a whole, the personality as a whole. It severs nerves in order to evade problems of blood-pressure and by cerebral surgery achieves amputation of conscience. Such shortcoming is at length being challenged, but the integral alternative — psychosomatic medicine — is as yet scarcely more than a name.

MECHANISTIC THINKING

The psychology of the past fifty years has been similarly defective. Repudiating the old "naive" conception of a "soul," it has split experience into meaningless shreds that cannot be reassembled into a living personality. Until recently, psychology texts began with a dissection of the nervous system. Then they essayed to isolate elementary sensations and feelings, which, of course, have no actual existence, and out of these bits of sawdust to assemble mind and personality, though usually there was slight awareness of functional personality as a whole in its integral relationships.

It is by reason of this deadly method that psychology has remained sterile save for petty purposes, such as selling more soap or capturing more votes. Not envisaging the realities of personality and society functioning as wholes, it has not got beyond trivial recipes for this and that. It has not built security for society or safety for the soul.

Religion itself, forgetting that God never made any machines, has succumbed to the blight and been likewise defective. Theoretically committed to integral regeneration, it has largely fallen back on "character building," or even on the Unitarian gospel of "salvation by character." Evangelical ministers seem unaware of the contradiction. Brought up on conventional psychology and sharing a mechanistic viewpoint, their efforts resemble those of children with Tinker Toys or Erector sets. The church has very little challenge to personality as a whole or society as a whole.

Twentieth-century sociology has become even worse than psychology. Originally organismic in a naive sense following Herbert Spencer's analogy, which treated society as if it were an animal, the sociologists have been shamed by the natural scientists and the psychologists into a mechanistic analysis. To them "society is made up of individuals," as if a mere population were a society. Accordingly they have tried to explain society by adding together the alleged qualities of individuals, as if unaware that society is the texture of human relations rather than the persons caught in those relationships. Society, of course, is a thing in itself, a tissue of relationships consisting of traditions, usages, customs, institutions, laws, and the like, which catch the newborn infant and make him in their own likeness; so it is much truer to say that society makes the individuals than it is to say that individuals make up society, but it is next to impossible to convey that idea to mechanized minds.

The ordinary sociologist, moreover, subscribes to the cliche, "There is no social problem; there are social problems," and seems satisfied with the idea of treating evils one by one, after the analogy of a quack doctor, without giving due consideration to the possibility that our culture may be suffering from a constitutional malady requiring organic treatment.

After all, mind and society are not mere engines to be serviced by mechanics. Something more is indicated than the tightening of bearings, replacement of worn parts, and the provision of new belts or connections. The new psychiatry concerns itself with the wholeness of experience, and the prospective sociatry will likewise regard society as a unitary organism requiring integral treatment.

MECHANISTIC THINKING

Most of us probably are confused by the ordinary tendency to identify "organism" with plant and animal life, whereas (according to J. S. Mackenzie's definition) an organism is "a whole whose parts are intrinsically related to it, which develops from within, and has reference to an end involved in its very nature." From this definition it follows that the mind is an organism and society is an organism, and hence that both require integral treatment as contrasted with piecemeal tinkering. Excision of parts of the brain, "the amputation of conscience," is a sorry treatment for anxiety neuroses. Cutting of nerves is a cheap makeshift in hypertension. Similarly, piecemeal social reform is entirely inadequate for the sickness of a civilization, for the death malady of an outmoded culture.

The finest mechanism owes its excellence to its approximation to an organism, and before we get our thoughts and our systems straight we shall have to get used to thinking in organismic rather than in mechanistic terms. We shall have to emphasize wholes, and to comprehend parts in the light of the whole. Thus we shall think of the universe as an organism rather than as a mechanism. Indeed God never made any machines and never will make any. Biologists are beginning to outgrow the conception of "the mechanism of inheritance," and to feature the pattern of the chromosome rather than the determiners viewed separately. Physicists are coming to regard the atom as an organism, the behavior of its parts determined by the pattern of the whole — just as a tune is not a conglomeration of notes but a patterned whole whose distinction consists in the system of internal relationships. Keep the notes the same but change their order and you have a different tune. Indeed a tune played backwards is not the same tune. A living whole is always something more than the sum of its parts, and the meaning of anything lies in its wholeness. This is true whether of an atom or of a soul.

Thus organism transcends mechanism. In spite of Henry Ford, no one has as yet produced a machine to give milk. No one has invented a mechanism to lay an egg. No machine possesses the power of reproduction. Indeed there are no piecemeal, fragmentary solutions for any significant human problem. Nevertheless our thoughts and our policies are still so under the spell of our mechanization that we try to reduce everything to gears and shafts and motors. We try to reduce everything to its lowest terms instead of raising everything to its highest power, and therein lies the futility of our efforts to overcome personal and social maladjustments. We even try to piece together mechanically a United Nations instead of giving the right of way to the integral problem of human unity.

Thus the whole framework of thought and action is dead-centered by our infatuation with our proven skill as mechanicians. The atom bomb is the symbol of triumphant mechanism. It will require more than pious resolutions by the atomic scientists to bring us in sight of a comprehensive, functional, integral grasp of the human problem.

That is to say, our so-called science has been standing things on their heads, and one cannot begin getting educated till he has got out of his system the habit of supposing that the way to understand things is to dissect them into their ultimate parts and has learned that meaning resides in wholes, and that parts get all their meaning from their relation to the whole. The whole is not equal to the sum of its parts, or even to the product of its parts, but is something more and greater, and different from any piecemeal result. The whole is the pattern that controls the disposition of the parts and determines their significance. Thus human personality as a whole must be the starting point in psychology, and if psychology needs knowledge of nerve cells it will get to them finally, in the last chapter, after it has learned enough about the general operation of personality to make sense of what it can discover about sensations and their bodily counterpart (just as the prime hypothesis of science is the wholeness of the universe).

3

ORGANISMIC THINKING

IN SPITE of the natural bias of a machine age for blue-print thinking, the better judgment of trained minds has all along operated along organismic rather than mechanistic lines. Even when psychology was in process of becoming mechanistic, the student was still assured that "all perception is apperception"— that is to say, we are not mere cameras, but whatever we apprehend is seen in the light of our whole experience and has an integral meaning. It was only a step from this affirmation to' the findings of the configuration psychology, which features the fact that we always sense not a summation of parts, but a patterned whole.

This is, of course, a common-sense fact, deeper than the unreal analysis of the mechanists, who talked as if one understood a whole if he had analyzed it into its parts. Everyone knows, of course, that a square is not the sum of four equal straight lines but a patterned arrangement of those lines. Even a machine is not a conglomeration of cogs, and shafts, pistons and gears, but an integration according to a pattern; so that the best machines, as for instance a rotary press, approximate the wholeness of a living organism.

No matter, indeed, how many pieces of anything we may have, we cannot put them together in a meaningful way unless we discover a pattern. Either we must know it in advance, or it must emerge as we shuffle the bits and fumble with them. Facts may stare us in the face without meaning, as in the case of the "hidden animal" in the picture, which at first does not stand out, but presently discloses itself as we contemplate the foliage among which it is hidden. Likewise a verse of scripture may be just words until we see it in its immediate context, and perhaps in the perspective of scripture as a whole. Understanding depends on getting every item into its entire context.

That is why the new psychology starts with human society, from which, like the "hidden animal," the personality emerges as we fix our gaze on the integral setting. Indeed the way to understand anything is not by mechanical separation into fragments but by integral apprehension of the organic wholeness of what we are studying.

Now, as we have seen, "an organism is a whole, whose parts are intrinsically related to it, which develops from within, and has reference to an end inherent in its very nature." When natural scientists rebel at the idea that anything save an animal or a plant can be called an organism, we need but ask why animals and plants are called organisms, and we shall see that it is because they fit this definition, and then we can go on to discover other things that also fit it.

Thus the mind is an organism, as is apparent when we place the mind face to face with the definition. Even Dr. Jekyll and Mr. Hyde are grounded in an underlying unity, with a common organic basis, and however much they may seem to work at cross-purposes, the case is no different from that of Paul, who found "another law" in his "members, working against the law" of his mind, even though we can discover no more fully integrated personality than Paul, with his "This one thing I do."

Likewise a society, say the Methodist Church, is an organism. Arising and spreading, integrating and re-integrating, consisting not of alien parts pieced together by an external process but unfolding as an orderly whole, with its conferences, congregations, funds, boards, colleges, and so forth, all inherently parts of the body as a whole, the denomination illustrates notably the definition of an organism. Its growth has come from reaching out and absorbing and assimilating to itself by an internal process elements originally extraneous. If there have been instances of adding on artificially and superficially, such spurious growth has not adhered unless it has been made part and parcel of the inner spirit. Obviously, too, the denomination has had a distinctive purpose, with its emphasis on man's part in salvation. Gradually, however, the inherent purpose has been growing into such similarity with that of other bodies that persistence in separate existence may presently prove schismatic, so that coalescence may be indicated. At all events the record has been one of organic development, not of mechanistic contrivance.

An atom seems to be likewise an organic whole, not stuck together, but expressing an inherent pattern and operating according to that pattern till the influence of

ORGANISMIC THINKING

a larger and more inclusive pattern modifies its behavior and its essence. In the same way, moreover, the universe as we know it answers more to the definition of an organism than to that of a mechanism. It was not pieced together but grew as the unfolding of an antecedent pattern.

The significant thing in any situation is indeed the pattern that determines its organization and function, just as in the case of biological organisms the original pattern of the germ (rather than the behavior of genes regarded separately) determines what kind of creature will be born and along what lines it will develop. The whole is not to be understood from the parts, but the parts from the whole, and until the pattern of the whole emerges, nothing makes sense.

During the present generation, science has begun, indeed, to swing to the organismic viewpoint. Perhaps the largest single contribution to this trend was made twenty years ago by Raymond Holder Wheeler of the University of Kansas in his Science of Psychology. For a long time the conventional psychology text had proceeded from neuron to sensation, to elementary feeling, to perception, and so on, with a possible ultimate recognition of personality if not of society. Wheeler, on the other hand, starts with society and finally considers the nervous system. That is to say, he shows us that discovery proceeds from the whole toward the parts; so that even if there is value in knowing how a nerve cell behaves, that meaning is a detail in the functioning of mankind, instead of mankind's behavior being pieced together

15

mechanically out of the doings of neurons. Thus even when we seek from the neuron light on the world problem of humanity, the neuron we question is not a mere bit of protoplasm, but rather a locus of human striving seen first in the large in terms of what we know about the universe.

The current attempt to establish on the graduate level a specifically Christian university expresses the awareness of the need of integral thinking. Scientists have professed to take nothing for granted save the testimony of the senses, as if piecemeal sensations could be summated into adequate wholes. In reality, science has taken for granted the patterns of human thought, never built up piecemeal at all but expressing in integral fashion the wholeness of experience. The new university will start with this wholeness of experience, which Christians designate as apprehension of God. So conceived, research would begin with what we are aware of in the largest sense as the wholeness of experience and would work down from there, expecting, of course, to enrich the total picture by elaboration from insight into particulars, but not supposing that a valid body of knowledge can be built by putting together items collected without any original frame of reference.

Scientists have, indeed, all along been sufficiently aware of the necessity of seeing the detail as an aspect of a pattern; hence their construction of hypotheses as possible patterns into which the discovered facts may fit. On the whole, however, they have not realized sufficiently that such a process is philosophy, and that they might better start with a general comprehensive philosophy to be revised and enriched as research proceeds.

16

ORGANISMIC THINKING

Now by whatever means, man has reached the stage where he consciously regards everything as existing for human purposes. Even the momentary consternation over atomic energy has not essentially shaken this confidence. Moreover there is increasing agreement that, whatever reservations are made in behalf of individuals and minor groups, the interests of mankind as a whole must have right of way. No atomistic, particularistic, mechanical formulas for a patched-together salvation will suffice. Thus for practical purposes the integral whole with which research must start is the unitary striving of mankind for fulfillment. What we know about this universal drive will constitute the initial framework for the new science, which will work out from there to an apprehension of a general cosmic pattern subject to limitless analysis however far below the electron, but assimilating all the new particulars as meaningful solely in terms of human aspiration.

So far, indeed, as our religion concerns this planet and its denizens, it appears not only that "man's chief end is to glorify God and to enjoy him forever," but likewise that God's chief end is to glorify man and enjoy him forever. Thus the most that we know or can know about the universe coincides with the most that we know or can know about the human race.

Religious leadership has too long been under the spell of mechanistic thinking. In spite of the avowed belief in integrality of experience and in the necessity of the rebirth of the personality as a whole, there has been widespread reliance on "habit formation" in the petty sense and on "character building." Evangelical Christians

17

have not had, in general, the hardihood to challenge the prevailing scheme of thought. Christian growth is not, as the mistranslation of Peter would imply, a matter of adding one thing to another, but rather a matter of enfolding and unfolding: "In your faith, supply virtue, and in virtue knowledge" and so on.

Protestantism in particular has exalted the fragmentary by overplaying the distinctness of the individual, as if society were just a sum-total of individuals, or as if the individual could be "saved" in isolation. We have lacked the Catholic sense of "the beloved community." Fundamentalists, specially, have made religion center in the individual, as if the general pattern of human experience mattered only as an exercise ground for individuals.

Of late, however, evangelicals are beginning to feature the necessity for social action, and they may even reach the point where they will prize, not the individual in vacuo but the individual as an aspect, a manifestation, of collective aspiration and communal achievement. The present Christian Amendment movement to procure national recognition of the sovereignty of Christ, however bound by narrowly political and legalistic concepts, is groping toward the idea that society as a whole is a fit subject for regeneration, or, as Canon Freemantle put it a couple of generations ago — "The World the Subject of Redemption."

Thus our whole outlook, our whole manner of thought is undergoing a revolution. No longer is it appropriate for biologists to picture the animal body as a machine; for such a crude analogy impairs the sense of over-all pattern, of organic wholeness. No psychologist today would say that mind is just a total of stimulus-response circuits. No competent sociologist would reaffirm Mazzini's doctrine, "There is no social problem; there are social problems." Even the physicist is prepared to explain individuality in the behavior of electrons by the pattern of the atom whose integral wholeness gives them their meaning.

Geometry, indeed, affirms that "the whole is equal to the sum of its parts," but no science other than mathematics can accept this dictum. Water is not a <u>sum</u> of oxygen and hydrogen. An emotion is not a <u>sum</u> of organic sensations. A community is not a <u>sum</u> of self-contained persons. The universe is not the <u>sum</u> of all that exists. If concepts are to be borrowed from mathematics, we might say, "Any whole is the <u>product</u> of its aspects," but even that statement would be misleading, inasmuch as here the "parts" are but <u>aspects</u> of the whole, to which they owe their specific qualities as involved in the whole.

In chemistry, for example, since many elements are seldom if ever encountered "free," in a state of nature, there is a tendency to regard the generality of elements as <u>human</u> creations, derivatives from the natural substances, instead of regarding "compounds" as put together out of "elements." Perfection of the science would consist in such a complete and ultimate analysis of everything that the formula for any chemical reaction would not be something to be strained after and painfully pieced together out of fragmentary experience, but rather an expression mathematically inevitable and obvious by reason of the subordination of the reaction in question to the over-all laws manifest in the constitution of reality.

Short of such a consummation, students have to halt and stumble — just as we all halt and stumble in all our thinking because, as automatic reflections of the machine age, we use the concept of mechanism as a pattern by which to understand everything. Once we have grasped the idea that a mechanism is a paltry product of man's ingenuity as contrasted with the organisms expressing divine creativity, we shall cease to twist and wrest reality into the stiff pattern of the machine fabricated from dead parts, and shall conceive of everything in terms of an overruling vital wholeness, which is what devout people mean by "God."

4

THE MEANING OF SCIENCE

IN AN AGE of science, such as ours is, all culture gets expressed in terms of science, and the malady of a culture undermines confidence in the science with which it is identified. Recent proposals of a "moratorium on science" indicate pointedly a paradox of civilization. Our knowledge has so far outrun our practice that on that score alone ours is a reprobate age.

The trouble, however, is not due to essential science, but to the fact that science has unwittingly succumbed to the mechanistic illusion to the point of assuming that causality is identical with mechanical linkage — an assumption that threatens, by its unsoundness, to lead to a repudiation of causality and to the assumption that some things happen for no reason.

One common error relevant to this confusion is the tacit identification of science with a field of knowledge or a body of knowledge, as if a sufficient localization and accumulation of information could satisfy man's intellectual interests or fulfill his scientific urge. Obviously the moron that can rattle off the names and numbers on all the cars of a freight train that has passed is not a scientist, though the train were a mile long, nor is he moving in the direction of science. The same would be true were his list that of plants or insects in a habitat.

On the other hand, the person who can explain how it happens that cars from such a variety of roads are to be found in one freight train is on the track of an order and a pattern in our scheme of transportation and is on his way toward its becoming an area of science; for in science it is the tissue of relationships that gives meaning to the data and makes them significant. That is, science is a viewpoint and a method, valid in any field; and it covers not merely what is known, but also what is believed or supposed.

There has, indeed, been great exaggeration of the sheer importance of mere data, the mere accumulation of sense testimony, as if the required truth would automatically emerge from the mere piling up of separate facts; whereas in practice, research always proceeds by the making of suppositions, the erection of hypotheses — conjectural patterns into which the observed facts may possibly fit — and testing these hypotheses to the point where, if not disproved, they become tentative beliefs — theories — and perhaps ultimately assured beliefs — laws. If the data do so fit, then they acquire significance and the conjectural pattern is confirmed, but always with the reservation that the findings may become outmoded and superseded.

Thus science is not mere reliance on the testimony of the senses (which reliance is itself an article of faith, inasmuch as there is no direct assurance that the senses really put us next to the nature of things) for behind the scientist's confidence in man's senses is faith in the meaning of the universe. There could, indeed, be no science save as the researcher has confidence that the whole scheme of things is not a trick. Belief that a consistent universe tells a consistent story is the first step toward science.

Scientific method, then, is not the mere contemplation of isolated impressions accepted as facts; neither is it the mere piecing together of such items of information. Rather is it essentially the formulation and testing of hypotheses, the primary and overruling hypothesis being that this is a universe, that it is consistent, and that it makes sense. Many a scientist may overlook the entire dependence of his researches on such an original assumption and may think that his only axiom is the reliability of sense impressions; but in so far as he is valid at all, he proceeds implicitly on these larger surmises.

So regarded, science is not a mechanistic accumulation of data, not an encyclopedia of knowledge, but an organismic unfolding of situations. From a genuinely scientific viewpoint, the whole is not be to understood from the parts, but the parts are to be understood in the light of the whole; in order, of course, that they may reflect back new light on the nature of the whole.

The initial hypothesis of science, then, is faith in the meaning of the universe, which in scripture parlance is to say that "all things hold together" and "all things work together." Unless one has this presumption as the background and foundation of all his thinking, there is no possibility of his being scientific, for science presumes the essential uniformity of nature under "the reign of law." It could not deal with an incoherent mass of mere information about odds and ends, as it would have to do if it lacked the assumption that this is a universe, rather than a chaos, and if it could not depend on the unity and integrity of the whole scheme of things.

On such a reliable background, however, science can proceed to more detailed hypotheses as keys to further learning. If, indeed, it be objected that science ought to deal in fact rather than in conjecture, the psychologist is able to assure us that in a field where one has <u>some</u> knowledge, a guess is more likely to be true than false, so that there ought to be a premium on competent guessing. Those objective tests, in fact, that discount the results in order to rule out guessing are aimed in the wrong direction. They try to tie the student down to what is known for sure, and thereby they discourage the very power on which science depends — the power to project the imagination constructively into an area not yet mastered. Furthermore, a general pushing of hypotheses is a more fruitful quest of truth than is purely disinterested inquiry, inasmuch as the rider of a hobby is pretty sure to unearth everything that can be said in its behalf, and so arrive the more certainly at a showdown with riders of other hobbies.

The key to achievement in research rests, thus, in competence at hypothesis making, that is, at philosophizing, and the brash nineteenth century assumption that science would crowd out philosophy proves to be a strangely myopic fallacy, as is likewise the notion that science is ever adequate short of the supreme hypothesis that posits the wholeness of things, which theologians call God.

Another common error of thought is the identification of science with a particular area of interest, usually with "the natural sciences." Even if it is recognized that science is only incidentally a body of knowledge and much more a method, it is commonly supposed that this method is of limited applicability, as for instance to "physical" or "material" phenomena, whereas if it has any value at all, science applies, as we have noted, to everything that can be known, everything that can be supposed, everything that can be thought, everything that can be desired. When Jesus said, "If any person is willing to do God's will, he will know about the teaching, whether it is of God, or whether I speak from myself," he was proposing a scientific experiment based on the positing of a major hypothesis to be tested by factual experience. That is to say, if there is anything at all in theology, the field will submit to scientific method.

But between physics and theology lies a whole range of interest that science has largely avoided, particularly the field of human experience, which has been left largely to wishful thinking. Now of course the natural sciences themselves are nothing more or less than an aspect of man's collective effort, and the study of them is more a study of human behavior than of objective fact. So much is this the case that there is now a pronounced tendency to regard "the laws of nature" as the projection upon nature of subjective patterns of human thinking rather than as apprehension of the inner nature of external things — just as "red" in the sense people mean is in the "mind" rather than in the object or even in the retina. At all events, the natural sciences are themselves social sciences, manifestations of collective enterprise in the pursuit of social interests.

When, however, science is applied to mind and society, a certain type of ostensibly scientific mind balks because he cannot see how human thought and action can be measured with exactness. Behavior seems indeterminate, incalculable, incapable of being reduced to law and order to a degree acceptable to chemist, physicist, or biologist. The real point, however, is that increase in complexity does not lift phenomena out of the realm of science, however it may postpone arrival at a comfortable degree of clarity and assurance. Moreover the revulsion against the conception that science can measure human behavior leads naturally to notions of "indeterminacy" in the realm of "natural" phenomena, as if electrons could behave in human fashion. Perhaps, indeed, they do, but the conclusion would not militate against causality, but would rather prompt more diligent effort at making psychology and sociology scientific.

Certainly the matter of hypothesizing, on which science rests, should be far easier in the intimate realm of human experience than in the objective realm of "nature." In fact, every notion, every aspiration, every social movement is a hypothesis subject to the test of fruition, so that if man cared to he could speedily enough become very wise on the basis of common experience. It may not be possible to arrange enough laboratory experiments in social action to put all human behavior on that sort of scientific basis, but, given a reasonable desire to rescue mankind from the current predicament, there is no reason why sociology could not, on the basis of past and current history, be made as scientific, as good an instrument of control, as chemisty or physics; for while these two sciences can manage material phenomena, they seem unable to steer the results in directions consistent with man's safety, or even survival. They too need to be made soundly sociological.

Moreover if we consent to a real social science, we shall have taken the necessary step toward a scientific theology, for the real issue of human effort is mankind as a whole in the face of experience as a whole, which is the quest ordinarily designated as religion.

In this field science applies as directly as elsewhere. Many years ago a writer who considered himself devoid of religion remarked that if enough credible witnesses testified to religious experience their testimony would have to be taken seriously, just as would honest testimony in any other field. Obviously the test of it could not be left to persons with blind spots in the spiritual realm anymore than could experiments of an ultimate nature in the field of vision be entrusted to blind men, but in general the technique for verification of spiritual phenomena would run parallel to that for testing hypotheses in the material realm. At present Rhine's studies in "extra-sensory perception" may not be taken very seriously by psychologists in general, but they point the way toward a whole range of investigation in the field of religious experience, notably in respect to such phenomena as "inspiration" and "revelation." In any event, the phenomena of religion can be checked by the pragmatic test proposed by Christ— will it work?

True science, that is to say, takes the background of Christianity for granted in that it builds on confidence in the "the uniformity of Nature." By its reliance on "the reign of law" it manifests faith in the meaning of the universe, which is the supreme hypothesis. Thus science— the formation and testing of hypotheses— is not a mechanistic accumulation of sense impressions but an organismic unfolding of integral situations. The whole is not to be understood from the parts, but the parts from the whole. Thus science corroborates the presumption of Christianity, which rests in the confidence that Christ "is before all things, and in him all things hold together."

5

THE USE OF HYPOTHESES

THE PERSON that insists on excluding everything save sense testimony is always unaware that there is no such thing as pure sensory impression. He overlooks the fact that the human organism always supplies part of the picture, so that perception is largely subjective; "all perception is apperception." That is to say, all we know about the universe is filtered through the medium of human personality and diluted or refracted thereby, so that its value is relevant to human experience. Every conception is thus anthropomorphic and anthropocentric and there is no possibility whatever of pure objectivity; furthermore it would serve no purpose even if it were possible.

In science, however, as contrasted with mere "common sense," instead of merely acquiescing in past experiences as an interpreter of the new perception, the observer deliberately and sharply focuses experience through creative imagination and explicitly says, "In the light of all that is already known, this phenomenon probably means that...." Such is the process of forming hypotheses.

In other words, science hinges on guesswork. Only by guessing boldly and then testing the guesses relentlessly can science advance. The better the scientist the better his hunches and the more the probability of arriving at truth. It is better, furthermore, as already remarked, if each scientist backs to the limit his own guesses than if everyone were all the time striving for sheer impartiality; for when each one is riding his own hobby, the utmost possibilities that it contains are likely to be brought out, and promptly corrected by the findings of others, according to the maxim of Paul, "Put all things to the test; hold fast what is good." Of course if one persists in holding himself aloof from and superior to the social process of collaboration, he is no scientist.

It will bear repeating that the validity of guesswork rests in the fact that in a field where one has some knowledge, a guess is more likely to be true than false, so that guessing ought to be encouraged, inasmuch as life consists mostly in acting on probabilities. In so far, indeed, as we essay to confine ourselves to certainties we stagnate, and in the advancement of science, as in the realm of religion, "we walk by faith, not by sight"; for the meaning of what we see is itself dependent on our confidence in the whole scheme of things and in the reliability of experience.

There is, of course, a certain danger to which scientists as well as ordinary mortals succumb — the temptation to flights of fancy too far beyond verified experience; but these are not serious unless we become so identified with our hypotheses that a challenge to them is taken as an infringement on our personalities. The real scientist has to be willing, is willing, to set aside the most cherished hypothesis, however close it has grown to his heart, when a rival interpretation proves superior. Bias is not unscientific, but it must be correctible.

THE USE OF HYPOTHESES

When, however, vested interests arise to insist that mere possibility has become probability, or that probability has become certainty even though honest inquiry would still hold the case open, science and morals suffer damage. It may be observed, too, that such derelictions may occur in the realm of ostensible science as surely as in the sphere of avowed religion.

The present reduced emphasis on the doctrine of evolution illustrates well what can happen in the process of scientific investigation. At the beginning of the century, evolution had passed the stage of tentative hypothesis. It had become well established as reputable theory, and most scientists held that it was already an unquestioned law, which some were willing to extend beyond the realm of life to cover the whole history of the universe, as also to govern all spiritual possibilities. The spell of the doctrine was reinforced by what was regarded as a universal trend toward the better and better, though the essence of the original teaching had nothing to do with moral judgment save in so far as moral judgment might itself be regarded as a product of natural development.

Some scholars in other realms than biology did, indeed, express misgivings, if not sheer disbelief in the conception of such definite unfolding toward such definite goals as the biologist seemed to have in mind, but it was not till war unsettled faith in spontaneous "progress" that evolution (confused with or construed as progress) lost its fascination. The generality of scientists would doubtless still hail evolution as a law, but their

31

relative quietness about it has lowered it to the level of a theory, and very likely the best scientific standards would once more rate it as a hypothesis still to be subjected to a gauntlet of challenge and investigation.

Meanwhile the biologists became a "special interest" group, their professional prestige largely bound up in the fortunes of evolution, just as at the other end the fundamentalists became an interest group whose dignity required the undermining of evolution. History seems to have played into the hands of the latter in that loss of faith in progress has caused a revulsion against the conception of social evolution, except among the Marxists, who see in the Russian revolution and the triumph of sovietism the present stage of the historic unfolding of the social struggle and the natural selection of fit institutions. In capitalist lands it has become once more fashionable to feature freedom of choice and randomness of change, to the discredit of what are regarded as the straight-line theories of the evolutionists. But if evolution is dislodged from the clash of institutions, the contagion of thought tends to discredit it in biology also, so that biologists tend to a becoming reticence, influenced partly by prudence and the fear of consequences.

In Russia, on the other hand, evolution is still the gospel, but a fantastic adherence to accredited dogma, which makes environment prepotent over heredity, has led to the outlawing of "bourgeois biology," so that life forms are under the necessity of manifesting the inheritance of characters derived from environmental influence! — on which the early doctrine of evolution rested, but which was unduly discredited when science flew to the opposite extreme with the hypothesis of the isolation (the virtual insulation) of the germ-plasm, a hypothesis rejected later in the march of research and definitely disproved.

Thus science goes on making, testing, and rejecting or confirming hypotheses, but, on the whole, with little sheer absoluteness and with a large dealing in seeming probabilities. Certainly the forefront of science is no realm of certainties, and here, as elsewhere in life, we rest our case on major probabilities. As soon as anything becomes sheer certainty it falls into routine and is largely dead lumber of technology instead of the live tissue by which science grows and extends.

Science as guesswork and adventure is obviously more vital and human and closer to the aspirations of the soul than would be the grim framework of outright finality that science seems to the amateur to be.

6

THE MEANING OF THE UNIVERSE

WHEN scientific method conforms to the organismic pattern it inevitably begins with the largest whole of which we have experience or of which we can conceive; it begins with faith in the meaning of the universe, inasmuch as there is no use of investigating what has no meaning, and the parts could have no meaning unless they manifested a regularity, consistency, predictability, dependability, contingent on their subjection to some overruling principle, some integral coherence, some reign of law. That is, the parts make sense only if they are in consistent relation to the whole. Not that we can first understand fully the whole and then proceed to examine the parts, but that we must have a general conception of the whole before we can formulate any problems about the parts. Thus science begins by taking for granted the essential regularity of the universe.

Thus every scientist is first of all a philosopher, in that he begins by assuming that the whole of things is a universe, and not a chaos. Without an assumption of the dependability of the whole scheme of things he would have no incentive for research and no possibility of conducting effective research; for if the universe were a pointless jumble, incoherent and inconsistent, there would be nothing to study about on any higher level than random gossip. Some subjects are still in that state. Most historians, for instance, proud that they deal with non-recurrent events, are mere retailers of odds and ends of information about the past, or at least do not take the trouble to exhibit the order than can be discovered in human affairs. They do not aspire to a science of history.

In most fields of human knowledge, however, scholars prefer to look for regularity and recurrence and to develop their learning in such a way as to exhibit the general principles manifested by the forces at work in their field. They make the most of the fact that the universe is a universe, that their specialty is itself a (smaller) universe, and they are beginning to try to show how everything relates to everything else. That is why there is so much insistence on the idea that the vital part of any science is not at its core, but on the boundaries, where it touches other fields.

Now philosophy not only assumes the integrity of the universe, but also presumes that it operates according to the principle of "cause and effect," or, in other words, that, strictly speaking, there is no "chance," no "accident" — that nothing takes place without sufficient reason for its occurrence. This is the presumption, also, of the scientist. Thus "freedom of the will" in the popular sense (that something could occur for no reason or for no sufficient reason) is to the scientist nonsense. Properly defined, "freedom of the will" means merely that every person always acts out his own nature — that nothing can keep him from being himself. Naturally his behavior varies according to circumstances, but it is always in complete correspondence with the forces that made him and the forces that surround him.

Thus the universe comes to a focus in each one of us, and for each one of us the meaning of the universe is just our relation to it. For serious-minded people the contemplation of this fact arouses a sense of responsibility. If I am "the heir of all the ages, in the foremost files of time," then the universe is depending on me, and I dare not let it down. That it is impossible for man to conceive of the universe save in relation to his own interests is brought out in the answer to the first question of the Westminster Shorter Catechism: "Man's chief end is to glorify God, and to enjoy Him forever." The theologian who laments the softness of the divine who inserted the second item is fighting against nature, including human nature; for man can never be so disinterested as not to think in man-centered terms, or so purely intellectual as to conceive of anything save in terms of human experience. Even science has to filter all reality through the human sense organs, and it can achieve no greater degree of precision than they make possible, no greater validity than they are able to mediate. There is great truth in the dictum of the ancient philosopher that "man is the measure of all things," and in the assumption that the first step toward a scientific culture is in the maxim, "Know thyself!"

When, however, it is alleged that the prime hypothesis of science is, and has to be, faith in the meaning of the universe, it is affirmed that science is necessarily theistic, for if we have a universe (rather than chaos) then we are brought face to face with that integral

36

THE MEANING OF THE UNIVERSE

wholeness which theologians call God; and if this
wholeness has "meaning," then it is actively dynamic
as is the deity of theism; for the absence of active
dynamic is the negation of meaning.

Once more we come to the understanding, then,
that science, whether explicitly and avowedly or not,
starts with the assumption that "all things hold together," as Paul phrased it. Not even the present meaningless talk about "indeterminacy," carelessly phrased
so as to suggest gaps in the continuum of cosmic
process, really means to dispute the interrelation of all
things and the interdependence of all things. A scientist
with any faith short of that would be fatally frustrated
in advance.

The idea is best signalized in Tennyson's poem:

Flower in the crannied wall,
I pluck you out of the crannies,
I hold you here, root and all, in my hand,
Little flower — but if I could understand
What you are, root and all, and all in all
I should know what God and man is.

Here we have perfectly expressed that faith in the
dynamic, the vital interdependence of all things which
makes it possible and worthwhile to develop science in
the assurance that no apertures will finally persist in
the seamless robe of truth and that momentary lesions
in her body will heal without a scar.

But faith in the meaning of the universe holds not
merely that "all things hold together" but, likewise in
the language of Paul, "all things work together." That

is to say, the unity with which science deals is not fixed, static, settled, dead, but active, dynamic, fluid and vital. That is, science studies not things but processes. Indeed science finds no "things" at all in the sense of "stuff," but only processes. In the words of Tennyson borrowed from the ancients, "All things flow like a stream."

This fact immensely complicates the task of science inasmuch as nothing will stand still even for an instant to have its picture taken; every picture must be a motion picture; hence the fact of relativity. Even the seemingly dogmatic finalities of exact science are all implicitly wedded to this principle, even though physicists may not have accomplished yet a wedding of traditional physics with modern physics. Everything depends on time and place and circumstance. Short of deity, the absolute is obsolete.

But not merely is everything a process; everything is an integral process or involved in an integral process. "All things work together." Even if electrons seem to possess individuality they yield to statistical measurement, which is basic in any realm to the determination of correlation.

If, however, all things work together, there is no warrant for departmentalism in science, or for that provincialism which resents a psychologist's making a biological discovery or a chemist's throwing new light on sociology. Scientifically regarded, all truth is one and the web can be lifted by any thread caught at any point.

THE MEANING OF THE UNIVERSE

Departmentalism has, indeed, been pursued to the point of leaving no-man's lands on the borders between abutting sciences, and only recently has it been realized that the most vital areas for scientific mastery are precisely on these frontiers rather than at the hearts of the several disciplines. Now, however, the universities are subordinating departments to divisions and developing master courses designed to give integral grasp of broad fields, looking, of course, toward teaching the integral comprehension of all experience.

But whatever completely integrates is effective religion. Science furnishes thus the essential cultural basis not merely for the common life, but also for leadership in the realm of spiritual aspiration, "till we all come in the unity of the faith and the knowledge of the Son of God, to a perfect man, to the measure of the stature of the fulness of Christ," For John begins his gospel with the assertion, "In the beginning was the meaning" and proceeds to identify this "meaning" with Jesus Christ, so that faith in the meaning of the universe turns out to be, from the Christian viewpoint, faith in Christ, in whom "all things hold together," and through whom "all things work together."

7

FAITH IN THE UNIVERSE

INASMUCH as the initial hypothesis of the scientist is the dependability of the universe, it is not strange that some have come to call it "the friendly universe," though of course such a concept is a projection of our subjective experience. If the universe is "friendly," then man can get along by accommodating himself to its requirements, but whether the designation is more than wishful thinking depends on insight and effort, and the approach must be organismic, for while a mechanistic analysis can partly tell how things work it can never answer the deeper questions as to <u>why</u> and <u>what for</u> on which meaning and value depend.

The first consideration, then, is that, as Paul put it, "all things work together," which is to say that we are part of a universe, not of a chaos — that wholeness is uppermost, and that the seeming clash of particulars is but seeming, not actual. According to Pope:

All are but parts of one stupendous whole,
Whose body Nature is, and God the Soul.

But Paul transcends this conception when he features Christ as the binding principle — "In him all things hold together."

Belief in God is, indeed, essentially confidence in the wholeness of things, in the integrity of experience;

and belief in Christ is essentially confidence that there is the possibility of spiritual identification with this wholeness, which is soundness, health, salvation.

If, as we have already observed, the scientist did not believe in the wholeness of things, he could not begin. Philosophers may speculate about a "pluriverse," assuming that there are disconnected realms, discontinuities of experience, but if such were the case, no one could know it, for whenever the several universes became the object of anyone's thought they would cease to be a plurality, inasmuch as his mind had become a meeting point for them. In any event, science at least tacitly assumes that any fact has integral relations with any other fact, however seemingly remote, and when statisticians argue that a perfect co-efficient of correlation may arise by "chance," they are really begging the question, and we may be sure that "there are more things in heaven and earth than are dreamed of in our philosophies." Certainly there are deeper connections than are dreamed of by such as object to all monistic interpretations as too simplistic.

Indeed those that revolt from the idea of monistic interpretation are guilty of superficiality. They are unwilling to search deep enough to discover the underlying unity in seeming diversity, whereas the genuinely scientific spirit is never satisfied till it has worked back to the principle of integration that correlates all phenomena, that in which "we live, and move, and have our being." All human problems, for example, go back to the fact that man is faced with the problem of survival on a planet of limited size and reluctant resources, and even the most refined spirituality is a reflection of this predicament, which in turn opens all the vistas of theology.

Scripture holds likewise, as we have observed, that "all things <u>work together</u>." Nothing is either inert or detached or discordant save in man's blurred apprehension, as (according to Paul) "we are looking at a dim reflection in a mirror."*

Thus science has no grounds for departmentalism. Every fact belongs in every science as much as in any other, and the scientist that forgets that truth is a paltry person. Difference in approach and incidental variation in method should not be allowed to deprive of a liberal education, as today it so commonly does. Moreover since it is psychologically impossible for man to be interested in anything save in terms of human interest, all science is anthropocentric and anthropomorphic; all science is an aspect of "the humanities," and, science never being pursued in sheer detachment, all science is social science, its subject matter being not nature but man's effort to accommodate himself to nature, to the essential requirements of the universe.

That "all things work" is actually a truism, for since science discovers no stuff but only motion, immobility (immotility) means essentially non-existence. That which includes no motion can never come within human ken, at least; so that <u>our</u> universe, the universe

*Goodspeed tr.

as far as we are concerned, is unavoidably dynamic, and will continue so as long as man exists. The corollary of course is that man can cope with the universe only by a policy of ceaseless vigilance. If one mark of personal maturity is to be seldom surprised at anything, that is because in the very nature of the case a dynamic universe must be eternally full of unprecedented changes, for which man must be prepared if he is even to survive; so that the key to essential education is preparation for adjustment to inevitable change. If cosmic dynamics ever reaches a stable equilibrium it will be after man is no more, and we are not prepared to face such an eventuality. Bertrand Russell may suppose that he is, but his confession of faith is mere words.

But science requires something more than belief that everything is dynamic. It is not sufficient to assume that "all things work." Even if we could conceive of a dynamic chaos, it could not exist for an instant without such a collision as would annihilate it. That is to say, we must presume at the outset that "all things work together." This is the principle that makes possible our confidence that the scientific laws that hold at one place and time give a sure basis for inference elsewhere at other times. Thus science is not ephemeral and transitory. Whatever is surely won holds good and does not become out of date. From such a vantage point of vision, it is apparent how little scientific attainment there has been as yet. Relativity shows us, to be sure, that everything depends on time and place and circumstance, but deeper than relativity is the assurance of integrality, in

Duane Edw. Vander Brug

the light of which we interpret time, and place, and circumstance. "They are but lesser lights of Thee, and thou, O Lord, art more than they."

But if all things work together, then every detail gets its meaning as an aspect of the whole and in the light of the whole, and the sense of the whole overrules any momentary impression of confusion, aimlessness, discord, and evil. In the words of Pope:

> All Nature is but Art, unknown to thee;
> All Chance, Direction which thou canst not see;
> All Discord, Harmony not understood;
> All partial Evil, universal Good:
> And, spite of Pride, in erring Reason's spite,
> One truth is clear, Whatever is is Right.

Not in the sense of appealing to everybody's taste or satisfying everybody's fancies, for overregard for the individual is contrary to the obvious nature of things; nor yet in the sense of presenting acceptable finality; but merely as a workable basis of procedure, a ground on which to face the future. At all events, no one has a vantage ground outside the universe on which to stand in order to pass judgment on the universe. When Margaret Fuller said, "I accept the universe," Carlyle was not overstepping the bounds of propriety when he said, "She'd better!"

It is at this point that sentimentalists err in their judgment on past, present, and future, whereas realists can get the proper perspective, as when Karl Marx amid the horrors of unalleviated industrial exploitation could

almly pen, in the Communist Manifesto, a panegyric
on capitalism as the deliverer of mankind from the
backwardness of feudalism. It takes, indeed, a sense of
proportion and perspective to make tolerable a universe
so prolific in misery as ours has been, a willingness
"to be damned for the glory of God," as were Moses and
Paul, but a contemplation of hard facts leaves no room
for universalism in soteriology.

> Are God and Nature then at strife,
>   That Nature lends such evil dreams?
>   So careful of the type she seems,
> So careless of the single life. . .

Paul, indeed, is not universal in his claims when
he holds that "all things work together for good to them
that love God, to them that are the called according to
his purpose." But after all, "good" is a human concept
touched in terms of human experience and does not stand
over against faith in the over-all integrity of the universe, which transcends details, incidents, "accidents,"
and even tragedies. At all events, science were impossible if the scientist held, or even suspected, that the "universe" is at odds with itself, in which event it were no
universe, and everything would be meaningless. The
scientist, however, can proceed on the basis that "now we
know in part," but he works toward the time when we
"shall know fully, even as also we are fully known."

Meanwhile we may observe that the only atheist
is the person that denies (not so much by word as by
deed) that this is a universe; for whoever recognizes the

wholeness, the integrity, in the scheme of things recognizes God; even though many may call themselves atheists for no other reason than that they have never been confronted with a plausible conception of deity. Certainly the anthropomorphic conceptions of deity with which most persons have operated have no basis in science or philosophy. Thus the Westminster fathers did well to insist that it is a sin to form any mental picture of God. The dynamic wholeness, however, posited in philosophy and science introduces us to God.

8

THE INTEGRITY OF THE UNIVERSE

WHEN we call the whole scheme of things the universe, we mean that it is characterized by wholeness, coherence, integrality, integrity, so that it has consistency and meaning.

Certainly we live in a realm of order and regularity, not a chaos. Human self-consciousness, human observation, human science have existed long enough to give a sure impression of the reign of law. It is not to be presumed that new forces intrude from nowhere anymore than that resident forces vanish without consequences.

Of course if we set God over against the universe as an external factor capable of intrusion, the story will sound different, but it is far more practical to apply the term "universe," not to our particular solar system nor yet to everything except God, but rather to the total of all that exists. Now of course a total might be just a conglomeration, but man has gone far enough in his examination to make sure that the upshot of existence is not that but rather an orderly whole that makes sense.

Some thinkers allege, to be sure, that the pattern that seems to characterize the whole scheme of existence is merely a projection of the workings of our own mind imposed upon the outer world, just as what we call color is essentially a human experience; but if such a human way of conceiving reality will work, it must possess the only kind of validity that matters. If we can put the universe into our orderly arranged mental containers, then the universe is orderly. If it were not we could not lay hold on it, anymore than Odysseus could apprehend Proteus, with his faculty of assuming all sorts of irrelevant shapes and modes. Thus it matters not whether we conceive of cosmic order as objective or subjective. In either case, man has shown sufficient capacity for finding his way about, as he could not do in a trackless maze.

But philosophy does not stop with positing a universe; it says that this universe operates by cause and effect, which means merely that interrelations are dynamic and orderly. Not even the new doctrine of indeterminacy, with its featuring of immeasurable relations really says anything more than that we cannot be sure that man will ever grasp all the ins and outs of causation, any more than people prior to the microscope would have been warranted in saying that man would never be able to see what was not then visible to the naked eye.

The question remains, however, as to the nature of causality. Essentially it is, no doubt, a category read into our picture of the universe from our own experience with getting results. When we push a wheelbarrow we feel the process in muscle and sinew, and that personal awareness is the essence of causality, which, by personification of non-human agents, we ascribe to all natural relations and processes.

THE INTEGRITY OF THE UNIVERSE

The mathematical statistician, to be sure, alleges that we need know nothing in this regard but mathematical correlation. To him his coefficients of correlation are adequate and no other causation exists. From his point of view there is no question of push or pull but merely the measurable facts of co-existence and sequence. It will be found, however, that such a statistician is at a loss if he tries to function in economics, or psychology, in education, or biology, or in any other sphere where he lacks intimate awareness of material and processes. His coefficients are not just manageable numbers. They measure something, and he needs to know what, for only in an understood context, in relation to an apprehended whole, does the principle of causation have meaning. If, for instance, the marriage rate shows correlation with the price of wheat, "why" does it? and how does it come that in some localities the correspondence is direct, in others inverse? Science has to probe deeper than piecemeal co-incidence, which is a poor device in fiction and worse in sober fact.

That is to say, the human mind requires reasons for what occurs. But reasons are psychological, and there is no way of conceiving of cause and effect save by implicit, if not explicit, personification of the "powers of nature." Accordingly our theologians call God a "person," though obviously this is a belittling of deity, for by "person" we really mean a human being. The scripture never calls God a person, and indeed it puts him far higher above personality than personality is above stuff. Creativity is a concept so far beyond human effectiveness that it is inconceivable; hence our reliance

49

on anthropomorphic interpretation in terms of human effort and results.

Indeed, for us the meaning of the universe is just its relation to us and our interests. Such a concept is, to be sure, unmanageably abstract until brought within reach as by John in his declaration that "in the beginning was the meaning," which he identifies with Christ. Because Jesus brings home to us the meaning of everything even a person with slight acquaintance with Christ can say with Richard Watson Gilder's heathen:

> If Jesus Christ is a man,—
>   And only a man,— I say
> That of all mankind I cleave to him,
>   And to him will I cleave alway.
>
> If Jesus Christ is a God,—
>   And the only God,— I swear
> I will follow him through heaven and hell,
>   The earth, the sea, and the air! *

Otherwise there is no meaning in anything, let alone in the wholeness of the universe.

"The Song of a Heathen (Sojourning in Galilee, A.D. 32)", in Edmund Clarence Stedman, An American Anthology, 1787-1900. Boston Houghton Mifflin Company, 1900, p. 478.

9

SPIRITUAL INSIGHT

PHILOSOPHY has commonly not been content to express itself in purely secular terms, but has frequently taken the form of theology, in which the problems of the natural order are related to the will of deity. People often confuse theology with religion, but the two must be kept distinct, for a religion may lack a theology, and on the other hand a person very competent in theology may lack the essence of religion, which is a social attitude toward one's universe.

Christianity is obviously a religion with a theology. That is to say, it is not merely a life attitude but also a theory about reality. The Christian is supposed to have intellectual grounds for his convictions and his loyalties.

In the first place, Christianity holds that the whole scheme of things that we call the universe is not an accident but a purpose. John begins his gospel by declaring that "In the beginning was the meaning." The theologian, moreover, carries this idea back to the eighth chapter of Proverbs, where the original creative intelligence is personalized as dynamically present in the process of creation, and forward into the interpretation of Paul's letter to the Colossians, where Christ is declared to be "before all things, and by him all things hold together." That is to say, Christianity finds in the person of Christ the meaning, the plan, the purpose, the creative intelligence, and the binding principle of whatever exists.

THE CULTURAL CONCEPT OF CHRISTIANITY

It must be apparent from previous discussion that a mechanistic analysis of reality is the antithesis of the Christian interpretation, even though most higher learning even in ostensibly Christian institutions, is tacitly and overtly committed to such a materialistic viewpoint and method; whereas only an organismic approach, yielding an integral comprehension, is reconcilable with Christianity. It would appear thus that most of science must be reoriented, reorganized, rearranged, if it is to meet Christian standards of tolerance; indeed that our whole system of thought must be transformed before our intellectual achievements will be reputable. Meanwhile science is in the position of standing on its head, or at best of sprawling in mid-air, quite incapable of giving us a workable grasp of the universe or of human problems in our age of crisis.

Christianity, however, has a cosmic philosophy, which, unfortunately, has not been implemented by official practice or by individual behavior. Thus while Christianity holds that the universe is not an accident but a purpose, our religion has not stood in the way of committing human affairs — man's relation to Nature — to chance and chaos. American prosperity, for instance, has been more a result of cleverness in plundering the planet, of brazenness in the gutting of resources, than of any constructive ingenuity. Now we have come to the point where American cities have quit trying to provide pure water, and have fallen back on medication. We succumb to a kind of blind fate instead of seeking the meaning of the universe in order to conform to it. Thus, again, we allow our atmosphere to be poisoned with chimney vapors and lead fumes from motor exhausts because it is too much trouble to achieve a wholesome adjustment to requirements of transportation or of industry. We are a race of amateurs in a universe that requires professional precision.

Christianity says, to be sure, that the universe is suitable to human needs. Indeed fundamentalists and modernists agree that man was made to fit the conditions of life on the earth and that there is no insuperable obstacle to successful living on this planet. The first commandment is not in the decalog but in Genesis 1, where we are told to be "be fruitful, multiply, fill the earth and subdue it." Thus the beginning of Christian duty lies in the realm of sociology and economics, which provide the key instruments for demonstrating the suitability of the universe to man's needs. The first part of the command, being dependent chiefly on spontaneous impulse, has been measurably fulfilled, but man is so far from cherishing the earth and subduing it that he has almost decided that it is better to kill one another off than to try to measure up to what the order of Nature requires of us for survival. Before man can effectively subdue the earth, he will have to go on from chemistry, physics, and biology to a mastery of psychology, sociology, economics, and politics, and to translate these sciences into effective collective living.

Some Christians presume, to be sure, that the mere presence of the grace of God in the heart will automatically eventuate in right living, but they seldom are consistent with this view, for they lay great stress on moral training, instruction in righteousness, which, however, is usually confined to the intimate, face-to-face realms of life. In fact, the church commonly disclaims responsibility for guiding its members into sound principles of collective living as manifested in the political, economic, and social life. It leaves the individual without a pattern for this field and trusts that he will unaided find his right relation to it and his right place in it.

Nevertheless Christianity does claim that we can find our right place in our universe, not by coercing Nature but by humoring her through conformity to her constitution. This consideration brings us back to the reign of law, the order of the universe, or whatever conception emancipates from superstition and reliance on chance. Man is, however, prone to an effort to beat the game. He ignores conservation and falls back on short-sighted selfishness. If asked to consider posterity, he says, "What did posterity ever do for us?" or bids posterity cudgel its brains to find substitutes. The farmer knows he ought to restore soil fertility, but pursues his old, wasteful practices, because he will be dead before the curtain falls. Our piecemeal, fragmentary view of things makes it impossible for us to seek integral solutions for cosmic problems.

So far, indeed, from regarding the material environment as adequate is our ordinary policy that we waste most of our energy in conflict over the division of a paltry product instead of discovering ways to integrate all human energies in behalf of a decent life for all. As

54

over against this chaotic waste, Christianity (which is not a religion of surrender, negation, annihilation, nor yet a religion of strain, tension, and continual frustration) insists on the faultiness of society past and present and sets standards of economy and efficiency pointing forward to the achievement of human adjustment on this planet — standards which are, however, commonly sentimentalized away or denounced as "counsels of perfection." Anyone seriously proposing a competent use of the planet according to an all-embracing plan is dismissed as Utopian, though of course Utopia — the co-operative commonwealth — is but another name for the Kingdom of God, which constitutes the plot of the Bible, to the advent of "the Holy City" coming "down out of heaven from God."

This compelling theme runs indeed from the idyllic garden of Genesis to the ideal city — a garden city — of the Apocalypse, and the struggle for justice which colors the narrative throughout is the spiritual expression of the revolt against oppression and exploitation, which is to go on till "the Kingdom, and the dominion, and the greatness of the kingdom under the whole heaven shall be given to the consecrated people of the Most High."

Certainly there is no point in human effort if it can hope for nothing better than the maintenance of the status quo. In the past century Thomas Huxley, appalled by the decadent misery of British life, declared that unless a substantial improvement in the condition of the masses could be hoped for, we might well pray for a kindly planet to come and sweep everything away. Since Huxley's day conditions have substantially altered but have become so much more menacing and frightful that hope in the evolution of sweet reasonableness has been replaced by a general avowal of human helplessness. Nothing short of a supernal faith and confidence based on an over-all philosophy sub specie aeternitatis can resolve the present deadlock of human energies and set man once more on his feet.

A mechanistic philosophy that tries to piece together a United Nations out of dead fragments, the potsherds of the earth, may create the semblance of a world order, but cannot galvanize the robot into life. An integral world view must be striven after and retrieved. But such an organic conception of the wholeness of the human problem, a conception calling not for piecemeal reform but for social regeneration, seems scarcely capable of awakening man's interest, let alone firing his imagination; for our science, our education, our whole culture are so wedded to mechanistic concept and method that scarcely anyone knows how even to look for wholes. An economics text, for example, is advertised with the assertion that economics is the only discipline where one must know the whole in order to understand the parts. Of course such a claim is absurd. For one thing, hardly any economists understand this necessity, or, at least hardly any are governed by it in their presentations. Moreover economics has no more need of organismic integration than has every other discipline. Religion is particularly at a loss in this respect. Sunday School lessons, for example, are mostly detached fragments, each pointing up an isolated idea, and there is very little attempt to get a comprehensive view of the meaning of Christianity. Systematic theology has yielded to random homilies closely related to counsels of expediency. The church has largely abdicated to the state, as is apparent in every country under war tension. In short, the essence of Christianity is accentuated by its general abandonment, even by ostensibly Christian circles. Moreover we may be sure that any possible recovery of a Christian philosophy will be involved in an intellectual revolution that will discard mechanistic concepts and get back to a soundly organismic presentation of the meaning of the universe as a function of the meaning and value of life.

Religion in general is indeed "a social attitude toward one's universe," but it is the distinction of Christianity that it professes to prepare man for the complete and final mastery of that universe to human advantage. In this light, there is no real distinction between the material and the spiritual, the secular and the sacred. Whatever is legitimate and important is sacred; and spirituality, far from being a compartment of life, is an attitude and a tone pervading the whole of life as an integral experience — the whole in subjection to the law of Christ.

10

THE QUEST FOR CERTAINTY

THE SUCCESSES that man has so far scored are in the realm of exact measurement, on which sound technique depends. Outside the area of "the exact sciences" man is a failure. Hence it is natural that thinking should have become mechanistic. Not that the exact correlation that we call causation is necessarily mechanical, but that we are most struck by its visible expression in machinery, which is more impressive than the subtler, chemical processes.

It is coming to be maintained, moreover, that success in the psychological and social realms is predicated on the development of the relevant sciences into exact sciences. We are told, for example, that the attempt to select personnel by interview is of uncertain worth as compared with the results of objective testing, and in the political field we speculate on the possibility of predetermining elections by the hypnotic effect of scientific sampling which will sway doubtful voters keen for the winning side. The fiasco of 1948 merely incites poltsters to keener efforts.

At the opposite extreme, moreover, we are told that research into the phenomena of nature discovers no stuff, and we are being prepared for the belief that nothing actually exists at all save mathematical formulae. It would appear that our attempts to understand atoms and electrons by imagining or by diagramming are misguided, and that we had better develop the ability to apprehend and be satisfied by numerical representation. It is as if the scientist were lending serious implication to the assertion of the Westminster Larger Catechism that one of the sins forbidden in the second commandment is the making of mental images of God.

Something of the force of this current thought trend is gathered up in the assertion that "God is a mathematician"— inasmuch as measured order seems to be the essence of the universe. That is to say, the "creating of all things out of nothing" is the proper work of a mathematician, as Lester Ward obliquely suggested in his stricture on the mathematician as one who "spends all his time thinking about nothing." (So little store did the nineteenth century set on the sort of precision which modern social science aspires to substitute for philosophy.) Since Ward's day, however, we have come close to a realization that his "nothing" is our "everything." That is, nothing exists save as it expresses itself mathematically, and in so far as we have not mastered the mathematical expression we stand baffled in the face of nothingness. Of course we have not yet reached a satisfactory degree of exactness in our measurement of everything, and meanwhile we operate partly on hunches, as when a professor, speaking of a colleague not greatly interested in statistical precision, said, "Ah! But he has insight!" More and more, however, we are insisting that everything must be brought within the reach of mathematics.

THE CULTURAL CONCEPT OF CHRISTIANITY

Is mathematics, then, the surest approach to God the key to the "riddle of the universe"?

We may begin the answer by recognizing that the mathematician is concerned not about "things" but about relationships, which he finds to be measurable and that mathematics is extending itself further and further afield in the hope that ultimately all matters of interest may be measured, inasmuch as measurement is the key to control, because what is not accurately measured cannot be accurately controlled. Of course too, any thinking is just the apprehension of relationships. It is one thing, however, to recognize a relationship, another thing to measure it, and in proportion as our knowledge is reduced to terms of numerical exactness we come closer to answering God's question to Job:

Where were you when I laid the foundations of the earth?

Declare if you have insight.

Who fixed its measurements, for you should know?

Or who stretched a line over it?

Mathematics should enable us in retrospect to come close to the answer to this challenge.

The mathematician finds, indeed, that relations are not random but measurable and he is confident that there is no room anywhere for actual "chance." Even the heights of idealized human behavior and aspiration are not different in this respect from the behavior of gross "stuff" or from the behavior of the electron.

THE QUEST FOR CERTAINTY

It may well be, indeed, that statistics hold the answer to all questionings and all problems. In any event, the seemingly uncontrollable by reason of unpredictability is the proper area for research into those numerical relations that will reveal predictability and control. Thus we may arrive at a social order as trustworthy as the order of nature and may attain solution of our baffling social and personal problems.

Exactness of measurement is indeed the key to control. Hitherto we have depended mostly on hunches and their accumulation into experience. In the physical realm, however, we have definitely set up laboratory standards that eliminate guess-work, and have extended the findings into technology. In the personal and social realms, however, we still depend on the "superior intuitions" of the "more sensitive" people, who manifest a knack for leadership. Just, however, as we now know that a gifted genius on his own cannot compete with a battery of ordinary men scientifically trained as inventors, so we are driven to the conclusion that with a proper development of psychology and sociology we shall be delivered from the need of "great men" and be put in command of the communal resources for development and progress. This development will, however, be on an increasingly mathematical basis, whereby guesswork may be increasingly eliminated from human problems save in the matter of pushing hypotheses.

So long, to be sure, has man been a prey to the mystery called "chance" that a widespread set in favor of the gambling process has become so well established that not merely in sport but in the serious business of life there are many that think life on a basis of certainty would be savorless. Thus they want to retain the business cycle with its giddy ups and downs, arguing that only thus can sufficient drive be maintained to get the world's work properly done. They want to retain the "profit system" because of the alleged momentum afforded by the "gambler's winnings." We have not yet vividly realized the tragedy of a gamble whose stakes are "the bodies and souls of men." We are not willing even to establish a stable currency with a fixed purchasing power. It seems better to leave old folks in destitution because the buying power of their savings has vanished, and to hand unearned fortunes to others who have cunningly converted their holdings into dollars prior to deflation, with its collapse of prices. Any serious attempt to rule out crude guesswork from human affairs is denounced as bureaucracy or communism. Perhaps that is what Lenin had in mind when he defined communism as a system of accounting.

Perhaps, indeed, that is the essence of it. A medieval merchant could enter in his daybook, "Sold Ramuglia some wine yesterday. I forget what I charged him for it." Today, however, business demands exactitude of record and reckoning, and while today's accounting is trying to adopt a language understandable by common folks, it is becoming ever more exacting. When the Federal Trade Commission began about the time of the first world war, it found that few even big businesses, kept adequate accounts. Today, however, the tendency is all n the direction of more and better numerical records, he tendency carrying over from mere bookkeeping into he farthest reaches of statistical computation, which ventuates logically in a general system of statistical ontrol. Everything is to be measured so that everything nay be managed.

A generation ago, Roger Babson proposed a statisical capital for the United States, where each major inustry should have a building devoted to record and neasurement, with facilities for periodic conferences of esponsible heads, the whole to integrate naturally into a controlled national economy without the intervenion of mere bureaucracy. Perhaps if allowed time nough the business system would gravitate into such an arrangement, but the calendar of world events has elegated it to the realm of Utopia, and we may expect hat the necessary certainty will be injected by government impelled by no abstract theory of state power but y the force of international rivalry working through ompetitive statecraft.

Natural scientists, of course, also seek sharper measrement of all their phenomena. Everyone knows that nathematics makes experimentation exact in process and esult, but it is natural to supplement experiment with tatistics as a means of keeping track of and assaying he results, as when the geneticist tabulates the various ualities borne by the results of cross-breeding. Without tatistical method, it would be impossible to manage he biological findings having to do with heredity and ugenics, but by statistics heredity can be precisely

63

measured and comprised in a complicated mathematical formula that would make eugenics feasible if we were interested in introducing it. We are happy to apply such knowledge to plant and animal breeding but still cling to romanticism in human affairs. We gamble on posterity just as we gamble on the exchanges. There will not be the same reluctance to apply statistics to the behavior of electrons, which will have to be kept track of in such fashion.

Now in the higher spiritual realms, "saints" have always craved certainty — assurance of "salvation" — and such aspiration has not been presumed to make life tame and flavorless, but the contrary. Why should not the certainty made possible by scientific eugenics or by scientific ordering of the economic system and of society in general be just as romantic a quest, and to the general advantage of all concerned? Why should we be more careful with electrons than with personalities?

Mathematics, then, as the key to all science, can help eliminate chance and hazard from human affairs, just as it makes laboratory experimentation exact in process and result, for by the use of measurement we can be scientific about things that do not admit of formal experiment. Herein lies the possibility of social science, which depends not on our ability to generalize on individual behavior, but on our ability to keep careful enough numerical records to enable us to draw conclusions from "the regularity of large numbers," as illustrated in the measurement of vital statistics and other natural and social phenomena. We do not know who will murder whom next year, but we can approximate in advance the murder rate in Kansas or the United States, and we can predict other things accordingly, just because past measurements enable us to project our curves into the future.

The same Roger Babson formerly advised his clients to sell when everybody was buying, put the cash in a savings bank and wait till prices hit bottom, then to buy and wait for them to rise. Thus canniness based on statistical knowledge would guarantee speculative winnings. Of course if everybody took the advice speculation would fade out because the process would be deadlocked by the reduction of spectacular fluctuation.

A larger case of the same sort was Babson's war formula which, worked out on the basis of historic wars, yielded a coefficient including areas, population, resources, school attendance, and the like, by which the outcome of a particular war was determinable in advance. This formula, applied in 1915-16, indicated either a draw or a German victory, so close were the coefficients. The logic, of course, was that with acceptance of such a formula wars would cease because, results being foreknown, it would be foolish to fight over foregone conclusions.

The entrance of the United States, of course, pointed the necessity of including in the formula a means of determining what nations would join the belligerents and with what potency, but the basic idea was in line with modern tendencies. A chain-store system will not open a store in a location foredoomed to failure. Exact measurement of the volume of traffic and of potentia business prevents such blunders; so why should statesmen not be similarly canny? The quest for certainty ough ultimately to rule out gambling by stripping the proces of all interest.

If, indeed, we are to "think God's thoughts afte Him," we should put ourselves in the way of participatin; by mathematical measurement in the divine foreknow ledge and so sharing in divine providence by way o social control of life's vicissitudes.

11

SOCIOLOGY AS PHILOSOPHY

THE COLLEGE STUDENT who said that Lester Ward's Pure Sociology had shown him the meaning of everything else he had ever learned was becoming aware of the scope of sociology, which is a comprehensive philosophy of life, inasmuch as all human interests take shape in relation to society. The student's enthusiasm expresses, moreover, a common hunger for understanding, which is continually thwarted by the piecemeal character of our teaching and our learning. Most of what is taught and learned is largely devoid of sense, for the reason that the data are learned in isolation instead of as foci in a tissue of understanding. Too commonly we ignore interrelationship.

Now those would-be sociologists that declare "there is no social problem; there are social problems" are accomplices in misunderstanding; for any particular social problem is such by virtue of being a symptom of some constitutional defect in society, and no such separate problem has any meaning save in relation to the whole tissue of the social fabric. If, for example, alcohol constitutes a social problem, it is because our society as a whole is constructed on a pattern of tensions that makes it natural for many individuals to seek release in devious fashion.

Sociology, that is to say, shows us the meaning of everything in terms of mankind's interests. There is, indeed, no possibility of our taking an impartial view of

the universe— a view that would regard it in any othe
light than as an arena for man's pursuit of ends centra
to human welfare. The universe can, indeed, have mean
ing to man only in terms of the historical collective ex
perience of the race, which experience has yielded the cul
ture in the light of which we interpret our further ex
periences. A world war, for example, is not analyze
objectively at face value, but is accepted sentimentally
through a haze of illusions about ideals, loyalties, and
responsibilities mostly irrelevant in terms of essentia
current values, if only these were sensed and understood
"Loyalty" has indeed been mostly a device by which in
dividuals and groups are led to do things at odds with
common sense and at war with living interests. It make
us subservient to fictions convenient to the custodians o
an outworn order instead of alive to the claims of th
present and the imperatives of the future. Thus mos
Americans seem still to believe that something is to b
accomplished by conventional diplomacy though no on
has proved able to express the alleged gains in terms o
man's essential welfare. At this point, indeed, sociolog
proclaims its present incapacity to control policy or t
interpret the results. Because society is not willing t
look at itself in the large, sociology has been virtuall
defunct since the death of Lester Ward a generation ag

A bona-fide sociology would indeed show us tha
the community, not the political state or the individua
is the locus of meaning. The case of the communit
against the state finds classic expression in Samuel's re
sistance to the establishment of monarchy in Israel, an

he claims of community as over against individual
nterest are dramatized in Moses' prayer that he might
be damned unless his people could be saved. The state
can, indeed, validate no claims of its own, and the
ndividual borrows his standards, his values, his interests, from some community (family, neighborhood,
sect, party, nation) into which he is born as a helpless
subject for indoctrination; and some communities insist
hat if need be he must die for its principles. This situation, to be sure, may be used to enslave and exploit and
pervert the individual. Indeed most civilized individuals
have a slave psychology, not venturing to assert themselves in the face of the overweening community, but
such perversion does not change the fact that an "individual" is an abstraction; he cannot disentangle himself
from the network that made him. The only hope for
him is that he may be born into more than one vital
fellowship, so that church influence may supplement or
offset family pressure, or an international grouping may
modify or counteract petty nationalism. In any event,
the individual gets his character as a focus of forces, and
his personality is but a resultant of social factors. Thus
a child of today may exist because Calvin and Marx
existed, so that his parents became acquainted because
thrown into the same community by the convergence of
Presbyterianism and socialism, and his personality may
be accounted for in terms of such biologic base and the
social influences built thereon.

In final analysis, to be sure, all culture is to be
valued according to its effect on personality, which,

though itself derivative, turns out to be the criterion of the processes from which it derives; but here, instead of talking of means and ends and regarding personality as the goal of society, it is better to regard both as integral aspects of a general unfolding process, just as in Christianity the soul and the Kingdom of God are correlate aspects of the same development.

As for the tendency to regard the political state as the locus of values, it is to be remembered that historically the state has been a device whereby a privileged class exploits society, a fact directly sensed by the prophet Samuel when he tried desperately to avert the displacement of community by the state. Samuel was not opposed to government, taxation, and public service, but he withstood the political state, confiscation, and conscription. Even in Romans 13, where Paul is usually regarded as a champion of the state, it is apparent from the Greek that he is not talking about "the powers that be" but about "rightful authority," which he describes in terms quite at variance with the operations of the Roman state, which was a Plunderbund, a conspiracy of national gangsters forming an international racket for the successful exploitation of society.

Institutions have, to be sure, the property of departing from and even subverting their original purpose; so the question arises whether perhaps the political state may be captured by society and made to serve a communal purpose, as is being attempted by the British Labor Party, which has indeed got hold of the state, but whether to a higher end than state capitalism and egimentation seems still problematical. Institutions have, indeed, a proclivity for degeneration, but whether the tide can be reversed and pointed toward higher good is at least doubtful.

In so far, at any rate, as we have an actual sociology it shows us that all science is social science, inasmuch as it is not the case of an insulated individual using his head in a vacuum but the focusing of the energies of innumerable people living and dead on the solution of problems of common interest. The keenest efforts of the greatest genius directed in isolation to the achievement of purely personal satisfactions would not rate as science, because they would be entirely irrelevant. They would, in fact, be a form of dissipation approximating schizophrenic paranoia. Even "idle curiosity," commonly regarded as the mainspring of pure science is misnamed, for it is psychologically impossible for any person to lend himself consistently to any pursuit conceived of a yielding no human values beyond the personal satisfaction of the lost motion. The mathematician who vaunted himself in the idea that no one could possibly make any application of his findings was simply too limited intellectually to realize that there is no knowledge not socially useful, and that no one can consistently function except in line with purposes borrowed, perhaps unconsciously, from his social environment.

That is to say, the springs of science are in community interests and needs, and any researches not corresponding to contemporary needs (as when Roger Bacon in the Middle Ages talked of suspension bridges, ocean liners, automobiles, and air-planes) are but idle words. Moreover science is inevitably a collective project, inasmuch as every scientist is dependent on all that has been and is being done by all his confreres, whether he is consciously aware of his dependence or not. Thus science answers to the scriptural principle, "We are all members one of another."

The present predicament of the world is, in fact, largely due to the failure to treat all science as social science. Great abilities have been diverted into divisive courses that have set mankind at cross purposes, to the point of impending destruction. The atom bomb has not yet brought scientists at large to the realization that their activities cannot properly be "things in themselves" but must always go on as an integral part of nothing smaller than the aspirations of the whole human race. Science subordinated to state policy ceases to be science.

Sociology shows us, thus, that the key to the solution of human problems lies not in unrestrained individualism or in unbridled nationalism but in world solidarity on a basis of socialization, which would take and administer all world resources and facilities on a basis of community pursuit of community ends. Sociology shows us that individualism gives no ground for individuality, but rather erases personality and culture in the competitive struggle, whereas the road to individual self-fulfillment and community integrity lies in identification with common human purposes as expressed in the concerted efforts of mankind as a whole.

SOCIOLOGY AS PHILOSOPHY

As long as individuals and groups depend on "beating the game," the tangle of insoluble problems becomes ever more insoluble.

Now religion, in essence a social attitude toward one's universe, is the implementation of sociology, and if the religion be Christianity it knows no temporal or provincial limitations, but amounts to a searching fellowship that will not be denied. In fact, the supreme evidence of Christianity lies in Christ's intercessory prayer: "That they all may be one, just as thou, Father, art in me, and I in thee, that they also may be one in us, that the world may believe that thou hast sent me."

If, indeed, we are to obey the command to fill the earth and subdue it we shall have to learn to get beyond working at cross-purposes, for as Ward affirmed at the turn of the century, human progress is in inverse ratio to the waste of energy in conflict and in direct ratio to the pooling of energies for the solution of human problems. That lesson, indeed, Jesus taught, and his followers need to become good enough sociologists to make the appeal for solidarity convincing.

Sociology, however, largely an American achievement, has, as already noted, made no headway in the United States since before the first world war. The conflict frightened American society away from the desire to see itself in a mirror and as a whole. Since then we have been living at cross-purposes, in a welter of confusion. Ashamed to give a picture of such disintegration, sociology has scattered its energies in odds and ends of research about fragmentary details, and has thereby ceased to be sociology. In upwards of forty years, no worthy treatise in sociology has appeared. Thus the failure of our master science to preserve and further the sense of integration, the need of wholeness, leaves American scholarship helpless today in a chaotic, mechanistic world.

A Christian culture would, however, show us the meaning of everything in terms of everything else, and it would convince us that there is no such thing as tackling and solving "social problems" one by one, any more than it is possible to build character by piecing together separately acquired habits. Just as the individual life needs complete reorientation, inclusive regeneration, so, in the light of organismic psychology and organismic sociology, society must be taken as a whole, and as a whole repatterned after the image of the heavenly. As a matter of present fact, less harm is done by faulty administration of social institutions than by the fact that we have accepted a pattern for society that magnifies the role of divisive and predatory forces. At the beginning of the century, football was abolished as too deadly. What was to be done if the sport was to be restored? Should the players be converted, moralized, spiritualized? No one saw in such methods a solution. The rules of the game were changed.

Generally speaking, Christian people see no responsibility for the rules of the game. They are satisfied with the attempt to play decently, or at least they rest in their bewilderment over failure to achieve Christian ideals. To attempt to get an honest agreement to pattern our social order on Christian principles so that the system itself will be in line with pragmatic truth is scored as chimerical. That is, we do not really believe in the vitality and validity and practicality of the Kingdom of God, which is the plot of the whole Bible. Not until we cease regarding the sheer individual as the sufficient unit of everything, not until we sense the reality of the fabric of social relations which gives the individual his human personality, shall we be in a position to start working on an integral solution of human problems.

12

THE SOCIOLOGY OF MATERIAL INTERESTS

WHATEVER our ideals may be, their attainment is on the whole contingent on the procural of the material wherewithal; so that, in such a culture as ours, the most spiritually minded person is about as much limited by material factors as is the most sordid. His desire to Christianize the denizens of Sin Kiang depends about as much on dollars and stuff as does his neighbor's desire to spend his time cruising in his own yacht. It follows that the stigma of being a "materialist" does not attach to devotion to the economic process but rather to the use of the results for mean and selfish ends. Indeed, since science no longer finds any "matter" in the old sense, the word "materialist" no longer denotes anything but the self-seeker, and if the would-be converter of the Asiatics is doing his bit in order not to be cut off from heaven for neglect of the Great Commission, he might as well be called a materialist.

To be spiritual is, in fact, to be completely cooperative in the common cause of humanity; for spirituality is not a special area of life or a special zone of behavior, but rather an atmosphere, an attitude pervading and governing all of life. It is thus the key to all values, including the so-called material. Now sociology as the science of integration shows us that the sole obstacle to the attainment of our basic interests is man's reluctance to co-operate. If the energy spent in conflict were sensibly directed, the whole human race could shortly enter upon abundance and security.

To too many, however, it seems possible to beat the game, and the resulting demoralization makes the game scarce worth the playing. Energy spent in conflict is a sheer subtraction from the quota of human welfare, and competition, in the everyday sense of that term, consumes and wastes the greater part of our potential. The laissez-faire philosophy, with its premium on sheer self-interest, is indeed a striking example of the mechanistic illusion— the notion that a sound whole can be pieced together out of detached and isolated parts. As over against such infatuation, sociology emphasizes the integral unity of society and reiterates Ward's conclusion that social evolution has gone on at haphazard long enough; it is time for mankind to sit down and plan human destiny.

The fatuity of our economic system was disclosed over forty years ago by Sidney E. Reeves in his Cost of Competition. Examining society from the viewpoint of an engineer he discovered that two-thirds of the energy going into the economic system is consumed in friction and lost motion— sheer waste. If we were as scientifically minded as we profess to be, we would long since have corrected this inefficiency, but the report in the twenties from the Federated Engineering Societies largely confirmed Reeve's analysis, and since then the waste has been magnified to world dimensions and now has to be figured in terms of atomic energy. We are economical and efficient in trivialities, but prodigal and destructive in everything that greatly matters. Nowhere is there wide-spread willingness to subordinate momentary self-interest to the collective claims of the helpless world.

This trend has virtually destroyed civic consciousness in the United States. Before World War I the citizens of this country were rapidly coming to life and adopting the weapons of direct legislation. The Great War, how-ever, created disillusionment and desperation fatal to constructive civic action. Still more fatal was the period that followed, when cheap cars and cheap gas gave every repressed pigmy the grasp of power and the elation of irresponsibility, so that joy-rides and "cokes" took the place of the bread and circuses that ruined Roman citizen-ship. Gratification was no longer dependent on public utilities, and interest in common concerns evaporated. The helplessness of the thirties aggravated the collapse of positive civic consciousness. A parasitic economic order taught the masses the possibility of general para-sitism, and economic and social morale surrendered. Thus when the second world war began there was little margin of safety, and now prosperity is permanently on a war basis, gutting resources in the hope of political advantage, and individuals of good will are paralyzed by a sense of helpless futility.

It is obvious, indeed, that the solution is only slightly at the disposal of the individual. As long as we maintain a social order built on the principle of "the devil take the hindmost," it is hard for any individual to operate on a higher principle without laying himself open to victimization. Economics is not a matter of individual whim but of social institution: "business is business," and to a very great extent, as in ancient Israel, "he that departeth from evil maketh himself a prey," or if perchance some personal advantage be gained, the result is very likely social loss.

Thus in ordinary times, the efforts of people to safeguard their futures by saving and investing are personal virtues but social vices, inasmuch as capital equipment piles up in excess of the ability of enterprisers to match it to effective demand, and depression ensues. The only reason our economy is not now in complete collapse is that government spending (with the accompanying inflation) has for fifteen years created a momentary escape from the penalties of an unbalanced economy which shows no ability to return to "normal" peacetime course. The seeming flush of health is a deadly fever.

There are, indeed, two ways of getting things — making and taking. Either we produce directly for ourselves or for fair exchange, or else we spend our time trying to procure by force or fraud or speculation what others have produced. The former is the economic way; the latter, the political; for politics consists in trying to get what we have not earned (or in trying to keep from being deprived of what we have earned).

The whole contemporary period points to the sociological lesson that politics is not an abstract contest in behalf of the common good, nor yet an abstract battle for place and power, but a conflict of group interests. Under what we call civilization, the political state has been essentially a combination of privileged interests struggling to maintain their privileges. As a prominent law professor has said, "The purpose of government is to enable the privileged class to exploit the rest," and in his opinion it would "be wrong to change it." So far as America is concerned, the struggle goes back to the original forcible appropriation of the continent's wealth, never created by the hand of man, which unearned wealth became a lever in the hands of privilege wherewith to separate from the producers most of the wealth created by them. Thus the average citizen equipped with mere ability to work, plus the ballot, is never able to offset the initial handicap, largely because he has been thoroughly indoctrinated by the beneficiaries of the system. Consequently the dead, dull pointlessness of recent politics. The formerly lively class struggle has been submerged and lost in the general enjoyment of a pseudo-prosperity, which was made possible by keeping the world on a war basis, with government spending accordingly. Even domestically, ours is a false peace, though there is no prophet to challenge those who cry "'Peace! Peace!' when there is no peace."

Under such conditions captains of industry eulogize leaders of labor and both preen themselves as over against a dying world. There is scarcely a rudimentary realization of the sociological lesson that economics will have to succeed politics.

Sociology, of course, shows us that economics is a

matter not of individual whim but of social institution, and, furthermore, that we are now at the mercy of a social system never planned or intended by anyone, a Frankenstein that has taken us unawares while individuals and groups were following the gospel of self-interest, which created the monster. Under such conditions, no amount of personal integrity or personal heroism will avail save as pooled with like virtues of others for the creation of a social order based on the principle of integral co-operation in a common cause. So much more important have our collective choices become than our individual decisions that there is next to nothing that the mere individual can do to raise the level of humanity. Indeed a population of saints or angels would find it impossible to run a social order on existing rules and principles with appreciably better results than we are getting. The first act of such a populace would be, indeed, to transform completely the rules of the game.

To the dictum of the law professor about the rightness of political exploitation a professor of education rejoined: "The American people will never put up with that state of affairs. If necessary they will tear the structure of civilization down to its foundation stones and start over rather than submit to such a set-up." Only time will tell which professor sensed more keenly the essential trends of the modern world.

At the turn of the century, with the general subordination of government to the business interests, the old Political Economy gave place to sheer Economics. Now, however, with the world plunging into state capitalism, the trend is in reverse and we are once more in an era of Political Economy, though the name has not yet been restored. The general confusion of government ownership and control with socialism leads some to fancy that we are on a potential threshhold of Social Economy; but stateism is the antithesis of socialism however much so-called socialist parties may blur the issue, and we are still faced with the task of securing essential freedoms in spite of the all-powerful state. We are blindly disillusioned about practical politics, but we are not commonly aware of the fact that politics is a device for a class society, and that "government of the people, by the people, and for the people" would be beyond politics, inasmuch as the interests of society would have transcended class interests, and community would have superseded individualism, which is always the enemy of individuality.

That is, if we are to focus human energies for the conquest of the planet and for the attainment of security and plenty, economics will have to supersede politics. Not that we shall dispense with government; but there was government before the political state. As we have observed, Samuel's struggle against the introduction of the political state was not the effort of an anarchist, but that of a believer in a communal society with a government serving the common good. All sorts of institutions have governments, and when economics supersedes politics, there will still be a government — primarily an economic administration of things rather than a regimentation of persons.

THE SOCIOLOGY OF MATERIAL INTERESTS

Such is sociology's answer to the problem of social integration in the realm of material interests, a problem fraught with meaning for spiritual values also, because Christianity, with its emphasis on personality, reaches beyond the state just as it repudiates individualism (which is sheer self-seeking), and leads to the prayed-for consummation — "That they all may be one."

13

THE SOCIOLOGY OF SPIRITUALITY

Sociology brings home to us the fact that spirituality is not a special area of life, but the whole of a properly lived life. It consists in conformity to a point of view that takes into account all the relationships of life instead of just some of them. Whoever takes a long enough and a broad enough view of life and lives accordingly is spiritual. That is to say, spirituality comes with effective attainment and development of sound relationships. Man's struggle for existence has begotten not merely directly utilitarian efforts and values but also aspirations and appraisals of an "idealistic" nature which we call "spiritual." "Man shall not live by bread alone, but by every word that proceeds out of the mouth of God." The enlivenment and the uplift coming from such an outlook and such a confidence have often made for success, even in the material struggle.

Sociology shows us, indeed, that spiritual interests are not ethereal abstractions, not mere fantasies, but embodiments of man's collective experience. For instance the Old Testament struggle of Jehovah against Baal was an expression in spiritual terms of the struggle of the Israelites coming from the desert, where they had been disciplined in solidarity and mutual aid, and tribal justice, against the stock of Canaan practicing a predatory, exploitative culture based on commercialistic greed

84

and oppression. The fact that the record is couched in religious phraseology cannot obscure the fact that the conflict was at bottom over everyday material interests. The justice that Jehovah symbolized reached to the very bottom of every problem. To the Calvinist, again, "election" was not a mere theological hypothesis but rather a token of his own fitness for even worldly success. Today the doctrines of Jehovah's Witnesses and the manner in which they spread suggest that it is perhaps an accident whether a particular individual joins them or the Communists.

Durkheim pointed out that a man's sense of a supernal power is largely a reflex of the social pressure experienced, only semi-consciously, by reason of membership in a community exercising social control. The individual feels himself continually restricted in undefined fashion (in addition to the conscious, deliberate mandates) and the sense of mysterious power begets a theology. When man reaches out after fellowship with this pervasive force, religion arises. Indeed, as Ames made clear long ago, religion is a social attitude toward one's universe, an attitude superior to that of magic, which essays to coerce the powers of the universe by mastery of correct formulas. Thus magic rather than religion has been the mother of science. Magic, however, is mechanistic; whereas religion is integral, organismic; and science can never come into its own until it is freed from bondage to magic, and establishes rapport with the wholeness of experience. Then it will be co-extensive with religion, which will be its working attitude.

THE CULTURAL CONCEPT OF CHRISTIANITY

The fact that fellowship is the essence of spirituality infused fifty years ago Drummond's Ascent of Man with its emphasis on "The Struggle for the Life of Others." Indeed when spirituality is probed to its heart it turns out to be essentially idealized fellowship grounded in the fact, as developed in Kropotkin's Mutual Aid, that co-operation has been the crucial fact in man's struggle for existence.

Sociology features also the fact that spiritual interests are thwarted by ineffective economic and political procedures that substitute friction and conflict for co-operation and fellowship. Thus the child is taught in home, Sunday School, day school, that mutuality and reciprocity are the law of life, but he soon learns that those from whom he received these lessons are operating the great world on a dog-eat-dog basis. The result is not merely fatal to idealism, but, according to Trigant Burrow, it is the main cause of neurosis in modern life on two contradictory principles. There rises, accordingly, the question whether we shall cease to extol the higher values or whether we shall pattern our social order according to them.

That material incompetence and waste is fatal to spirituality appears amply in the history of the rural church. Whether fertility gives huge yields conducive to absentee landlordism, or whether soil erosion impoverishes areas and drives away a discouraged population, defective economics kills the vitality of religion in the countryside, and the rural parish dwindles. Some denominations, accordingly, have begun to finance family arm purchase in order to develop an assured basis for the rural congregation, which has hitherto been regarded as the main source of ministers.

It is sometimes, to be sure, remarked that prosperity is the Old Testament blessing, but adversity the blessing of the New, without note of the fact that the Old Testament is the period when Israel had some opportunity to build her own pattern of life, whereas in the New Testament period the world was subject to the universal gangsters' racket — the Roman Empire — so that decency had no chance to build toward general welfare. Under such conditions, spirituality was naturally a material handicap, as indeed it often was even in ancient Israel in the life-and-death struggle with Baal — that is Mammon.

There is no ground, however, for the common notion that adversity is to be welcomed as favorable to spirituality. The best example of a wholesome sequence in such matters is found in the Book of Joel, where a restoration of material prosperity is promised, after which "I will pour out my spirit upon all flesh; and your sons and your daughters shall prophesy, your old men shall dream dreams, your young men shall see visions: and also upon the servants and upon the handmaids in those days will I pour out my spirit." Thus the solution of material problems is a natural preliminary to higher spiritual achievements. Thus spirituality is a proper objective of social policy.

Moreover, spiritual interests constitute an effective dynamic for the solution of all human problems, simply because they take a universal view and develop a universal attitude, in contemplation of eternity, and that is the range that sociology has to cover in contemplating the integration of man's efforts. Anything less than such a boundless outlook and attitude is fatally defective, for when a narrowing of interests begins there is no end to it, as is brought out in a remark by Jean Paul Friedrich Richter to the effect that if we begin by putting the interest of our country above the interest of humanity, we shall go on to put region above country, neighborhood above region, family above neighborhood, and, finally, self-interest above everything else. Such degeneracy is obviously the reverse of Christianity, which, beholding "the whole creation" groaning and struggling "in pain together until now," waiting "for the manifestation of the sons of God" undertakes to bring to pass the time when "creation itself will be delivered from the deadly bondage into the glorious liberty of the children of God."

It was, indeed, under spiritual auspices that the Hebrew people escaped from bondage and essayed to achieve a free commonwealth. It was the spiritually minded prophets that continually called them back to sound social principles and revived the struggle for justice. Jeremiah, indeed, identified the knowledge of God with social righteousness.

It was, furthermore, the spiritual dynamic released by Jesus that so threatened the collapse of the Roman imperial racket that the gangsters had to turn and capture the church in order to subvert it to their purposes. The resultant eclipse of spirituality has left society ever since a prey to exploitation not seriously threatened even by church reforms, which must be far more incisive and sweeping than they ever have been if they are to regain for us the level set by Jesus and his apostles, not to speak of the "greater works" to which he challenged.

In a limited way, Puritanism did, to be sure, provide an effective dynamic for the conquest of society — by the successful business-man. Likewise Wesleyanism restored a degree of self-respect to the masses, even within a framework of control by the capitalists. As yet, however, we have no spiritual force to cope with the urgent realities of a crumbling world order. Even communism, as a secular religion, has been submerged by Stalin's state capitalism, and the world labor movement has lost its human dynamic. It has, indeed, become a prop for capitalism. Under such conditions, religious fervor is largely abstract and devoid of focus, far indeed from hastening "the glorious liberty of the children of God."

Sound spirituality may, indeed, energize all manner of human effort. Unfortunately a misguided spiritual enthusiasm may make people docile slaves, willing instruments for the exploiter. People even interpret the book of Philemon to that end, rather than according to the assumption that it illustrates a usage of the early church whereby the claim on Onesimus was by no master but by the church that had emancipated him from slavery and put him under obligation to work out his purchase price so that the freedom of another could be bought. "Where the Spirit of the Lord is, there is liberty."

The first step in recovery for us to take is through

return to the realization that religion is the whole of life. As long as we make an antithesis between religion and economics, religion and ethics, religion and workaday realities, we are sterilizing religion and deadening life. Every human problem is a matter of religion. Thus the present law recognizing only "religious" conscientious objectors is fatuous in that it means virtually "theological objectors," though theology is but a set of symbols for religion, and the objectors on "political" or "social" grounds are as likely to be religious as are the objectors on the grounds of formal theology. At all events a man's convictions are to be reverenced because they are his, not because some one else grants them a technical label; and to disregard them is to trample on personality, which comes close to being the unpardonable sin.

After we have identified religion with the whole of life, the next step is a realization that our collective choices are as sacred as our personal choices, so that public policy is as essential a sphere for spiritual emphasis as is the individual conscience. Furthermore the claims of Christ are not satisfied by procuring individual regeneration and trusting to those of right heart to save the world. Such persons require intelligent guidance in the broad fields of activity, for Christianity has as exacting imperatives for the structure and workings of corporations, parties, governments, as it has for private behavior. Indeed the bulk of scripture has to do with collective rather than with individual religion, and it is just as central to the claims of Christianity that society officially should exalt Christ as that the individual should claim him as the Lord of his life. The notion that Christianity claims only the individual is a device for turning business, government, society over to the devil, for no number of separate private choices can add up to a Christian pattern for society. The notion that they can is mechanistic and futile and opens the way to secular totalitarianism.

Our third step must be to pattern the social order with a view solely to the free development and the equal welfare of all concerned. The notion that individuals may be left free to put self or family or nation first is the antithesis of Christianity, which would shape everything to the needs of a common humanity. Indeed the slogan "From each according to his ability; to each according to his need" is the best paraphrase of essential Christianity, and it is too bad that it has been surrendered to persons aloof from organized Christianity. Not until Christendom concentrates on the realization of that ideal through a patterning of the economic system and of the social order according thereto shall we have convincing evidence of Christianity.

14

THE USE OF HISTORY

SOCIOLOGY studies essentially what scholars call "a field situation." That is to say, any social occasion, any social problem, is determined by the interaction of contemporary forces whose resultant determines a line of change. No outcome can ever be anything but the integral consequence of the operative factors.

Some specialists have been led by this consideration to despise history as irrelevant, but they overlook the fact that one is not likely to be able to understand and measure adequately the contemporary "forces" unless he knows how they came to be and from precisely what direction. Nothing can be described as at a standstill — without regard to origin and trend. Thus most sociologists have a proper regard for history.

They may be exasperated, however, by the fact that many of the most vocal of the professional historians have such an exaggerated regard for mere events that their history is little more than glorified gossip. The historian that exults in "the uniqueness of events" is glorying in the unimportant, for the course of history is a matter of the evolution of social forces, with the event merely a point in this stream. The characteristic occurrence is what matters, and before the "unique event" can be used in scholarly fashion, it must be resolved into a mere expression of the moving factors.

THE USE OF HISTORY

Such is notably the case with the great personage. He means nothing in a scholarly history save as he can be explained in terms of his heredity and his environment. In any case his importance has been vastly exaggerated, as is made clear, for instance, by Ogburn's study of the incidence of inventions. Great discoveries occur simultaneously at the hands of persons working independent of one another. That is to say, when by reason of social developments the time is ripe, the innovation bursts forth, and, at least in as well-knit a culture as the world now possesses, we need pay little attention to the "isolated genius." In so far as he is isolated he is sterile, and in so far as he is not isolated he is not indispensable. We can hire men to grind out all the inventions and discoveries we need, and what they do will be only incidentally their product.

If the world ever produced, or depended on, men properly to be considered "great," it no longer does; and naturally enough, now that we understand, and could have command of, the workings of the social forces. In any event, the closer we get to the "great man" the more ordinary he seems, according to the old proverb that "no man is a hero to his valet." Wells is right in saying that the ideally written history would contain no proper names.

Emerson says that "the use of history is to give value to the present hour and its duty." Certainly no one can measure completely any situation without knowing fully the meaning resident in current factors by reason of their history. The past is never dead, and when we resent "the dead hand of the past" we are really rebelling against the past's persistent vitality. Accordingly we are unable to manage the present save in terms of the past.

Thus a people ignorant of its past is in the same predicament as a person suffering from amnesia. He may be hearty and vigorous, skillful and competent, capable of large output with commensurate earning, but he is hauntingly distressed till he learns his past, his name, his relationships. In like manner, no one is a good citizen if he has no historical background, or a good Christian if he is ignorant of the history of Christianity. There is, indeed, reason for insisting on the teaching of history.

It must, however, be a different sort of teaching than has hitherto prevailed. Mere awareness of innumerable events in a framework of time is unavailing. No mass of mere facts can ever be totalled into a working command of history. What matters is the dynamic interrelationship that constitutes the ongoing fabric of society. Names and dates have no more than casual importance, and to exalt them into values is the same sort of fallacy as is perpetrated by the Sunday School teacher who finds some sort of sanctity in the distance from Jerusalem to Jericho or in precise figures for the cost of the Temple.

The Bible is a different sort of history. It is a kaleidoscopic drama of the origin, development, and triumph of the Kingdom of God on earth, and all details get their meaning in the relation to the procession

94

rom the idyllic garden to the ideal city. In this per-
pective our religion emerges as essentially the struggle
or social justice and mutuality as the setting for vital
pirituality. On this background one will not make the
mistake of imagining that the spiritual is a part of
ife, or that salvation is "an individual matter."

Unfortunately there is a general disposition to re-
ect scripture, particularly the Old Testament. We are
old that our faith centers in a person — as if we could
ightly apprehend Christ save in terms of the march of
he centuries. The superficiality of much of current
Christianity stems certainly from a vast neglect of the
meaning of Hebrew and early Christian history. If we
new Moses and the prophets, if we knew the early church
n its relation to the Roman imperial racket, our religion
ould become revolutionary instead of the sedative sig-
alized by the universal cliche, "How I enjoyed that
ermon!"

The writer of Hebrews sensed this point in his cul-
mination of a rapid historical survey: "These all died
n faith, not having received the fulfillment of the
promise, God having provided some better thing for us,
hat they without us should not be made complete."

The momentum of history can indeed be made
momentous for the elevation of collective morale. Job
Harriman, the brilliant Los Angeles attorney who led
n the establishment of the New Llano co-operative col-
ny, reported that at an early stage the leaders were
esperate because of the vulgar and vicious selfishness
rought in from the outer world, until they devised a

course teaching the origin of the universe, of man, o
society, and the whole course of social evolution since
all leading up to a realization that we are "those upon
whom the end of an age has come" and that we canno
decently let the universe down. Mr. Harriman said tha
this indoctrination worked. If I am "the heir of all th
ages, in the foremost files of time," I can hardly betray
eternity!

"Sub specie aeternitatis!" Pragmatism rests its cas
on what will work, but the legitimate answer is, "Fo
how long?" The rise and fall of nations is still th
enigma of history. Just why cannot a people rising from
less to more move permanently from better to better
Must every nation go through a life cycle to the grave

It is to be remembered, of course, that the history
of culture is like a torch race, with the light ever ad
vanced by relays. Now, however, we have reached th
point where we are in danger of deliberately quenching
irretrievably the light that we have. "If the light tha
is in you be darkness, how great is that darkness!" I
history ends with us, what thereafter? Our ancestor
talked much of "the end of the world" and were dis
turbed by imaginings of a flaming planet. Our father
softened the portent into "the end of the age," but now
the atomic bomb has carried us back with enhanced
vividness to the grimmer vision. How feasible is it to
contemplate on this background a return to "sweet rea
sonableness" that might renew the vista of history a
far into a brightening future as we could care to con
template? What is involved in Peter's vision of the
"new heaven and new earth wherein dwelleth righteous
ness"?

15

THE ROLE OF PSYCHOLOGY

CONSIDERING all things, as we do, in terms of human interest and human behavior, and recognizing that all human problems are problems of behavior, we are led to psychology as a key to the interpretation of all that concerns us. Psychology, again, is not a special compartment of experience, as is commonly supposed; as, for instance, when we are told, "That is not an economic problem; it is psychological" — as if there were any economic matters outside human conduct, which falls of course within the jurisdiction of psychology. All economics and all sociology and all science are psychological, and psychology is a necessary tool for the attacking of all problems.

All psychology, however, is social psychology. The separateness of the individual is a material separateness, a biological separateness, and when we think of the individual as the unit of anything, we are really, however unwittingly, governed by the fact that we can see the distinct separateness of his body. If we could photograph his mind, it would appear as a tissue of ramified relationships reaching boundlessly in all directions but so interwoven with other minds that there would be no possibility of disentangling the network without destroying it.

Thus the individual is not the start of anything, the unit of anything save the census. The child owes his

existence and his hereditary make-up to the fact tha
certain social circumstances brought his parents togethe
All the impressions that build on this foundation an
contribute to the unfolding of personality are eithe
directly social in origin or are refracted by the socia
medium through which they pass. The newborn chil
is caught by the network of two billion other huma
beings, who had themselves been previously caught i
like fashion, and is made according to pattern, the onl
variety consisting in the fact that no two persons ar
subject to exactly the same combination of circumstance
Everyone, however, gets his personality from the socia
contacts that germinated him and that nurture him. Th
avenues of expression that signalize the personality ar
likewise social or determined by social circumstance
There is no "individual as such" and the most "individ
ual" psychology conceivable is as highly social as an
other.

The individual is, accordingly, to be understoo
in his social context, without which there would be n
individual, and all his behavior is social behavio
That is to say that there is no possibility of doing any
thing that does not express the influence of innumerabl
other persons living and dead. Even the schizophreni
who is in process of complete withdrawal from societ
never escapes completely from the consequences of hi
social upbringing, however vegetal his residual existenc
may seem to be.

Society equips us, that is, with a personality, whicl
constitutes the general background and pattern for late

ehavior, so that the study of psychology is primarily
he study of personality, and only incidentally the
tudy of the elementary sensations and feelings, not to
peak of the glands and neutrons which are the physio-
ogical correlates of behavior. Such is the viewpoint of
he organismic psychology, which does not expect to
nderstand mind by piecing together dissected fragments
f experience, but undertakes, rather, to understand the
etails in the light of the whole. One understands an
ct, a thought, an emotion, not in itself, but on the
ackground of the complete life experience, not merely
f the person, but of the society.

Popular theology, indeed, talks as if the "soul"
ere a thing, a sort of sealed package of personality.
ropagandists, religious and secular, try to appeal to
he "individual as such," but of course never succeed.
ndeed it is noteworthy, even though paradoxical, that
he most ardent champions of personal religion and
f the key role of the individual are the most prone of
ligionists to resort to mass evangelism which creates
stampede psychology amid which no "individual"
cision is possible.

Such a situation seems anomalous, yet even when
e take someone aside, when we convey him into isola-
on, when we swear him to secrecy, or even when he
kes himself off into utter separation from the world,
ny decision he makes is just as truly social as if he
elded to a stampede. There is no possible way by
hich there can be purely individual decision.

It follows, accordingly, that fundamentalism,

which rests Christianity on the individual, is a delusio
in so far as it treats the soul as an insulated package i
a vacuum. In practice it seldom goes to such an illusor
extreme, for it cannot get around the fact that a perso
is essentially a nexus of social relationships, and is sig
nificant in and through such relationships.

Genuine evangelism, however, would address itsel
to society and challenge the group to decide collectivel
for Christ, knowing that it is the social fabric tha
gives meaning and value to life, a fact always realize
in the insistence that the Christian must needs becom
part of a Christian fellowship. It would be psychologi
cally simpler and sounder to strive for such a Christiar
ization of our collective choices, our public policies, a
would create the maximum probability of sound ir
dividual development and decision.

We need to realize that the socially-determine
personality is the necessary background for the study c
behavior. Thus the first chapter of a sound psycholog
would be Human Society, with an insistence that societ
is not "made up of individuals" but of relationship pa
terns and actual relations. The second chapter would l
Man in Society, and would study collective behavic
The third chapter would be Personality as a Socia
Product. Then would come The Personality in Societ
Only after these preliminaries were settled would tl
author chart Personality as an Integral Whole, and the
would come an outline of behavior, beginning with tl
largest aspects and coming down finally through pe
ception, sensation, and the like to the workings of tl

glandular and the nervous system, and perhaps to cell functioning. This is the upending of psychology called or in an earlier chapter.

The point is that we can understand the items of behavior only on the background of the largest wholes. What passes even for individual pathology is always social pathology, and while it may be necessary to administer emergency treatment to distraught individuals, there is no solution through the building of more and more clinics and hospitals. Short of a sane social order there is no way of avoiding individual neurosis. As the skilled social worker of a generation ago was quick to admit of "cases" in general, "We can't pull them out as fast as more fall in."

The same principle applies in the realm of religion. Everyone will admit that without the Christian family, evangelization is severely handicapped; but the influence of business and government today overwhelms the family, so that we cannot do much for the generality of individuals except as we provide a suitable social environment as a basis for procedure.

It is clear, however, that the prevailing tone of a community is never set by the majority, but always by a strong and resolute minority, in whose leadership the masses acquiesce. Thus to have a "Christian nation" in the practical sense means simply the effective leadership of a consecrated group. The Stalinists have made this psychological principle effectively operative in their way and for their purposes, and it will be strange if Christians shrink from like decisiveness.

THE CULTURAL CONCEPT OF CHRISTIANITY

Today, when so many are afflicted with neuroses, it is important to be able to trace them back to long-past experiences, remembered or, very likely, forgotten. This is the work of the psychoanalyst, who by exposing the roots of a maladjustment gives it a chance to evaporate, or at least brings it within reach of curative treatment. It is obvious, however, that we can never afford prolonged psychoanalysis for the multitude; hence the importance of reshaping the pattern of our social order to the point where it will strengthen personality instead of warping or undermining it. Society itself needs to be psychoanalyzed. That is, we need collectively to know the reason for our prejudices, for our antagonisms, for our susceptibility to crazes and manias. We need to know just why nations professing to love peace choose war. Until society is released from its obsessions, there is no possibility of releasing human energies for the completion of the task of mastering Nature for the common good.

Meanwhile it is futile to look for wholesale benefit from any psychology that hinges on the mere individual. The distraught person may be made more comfortable in a deadly situation, but no number of such evasions can constitute a tolerable, not to say a Christian, social situation. Anything done for the individual must always be done for the individual-in-society, and cannot be notably better than the quality of that society. Something is accomplished when a group of votaries call forth a "little flock" as a reciprocal zone of safety, but nothing short of a social commonwealth of mutuality —

the Kingdom of God — offers a reasonable hope of "the wholesome personality" or of defensible "peace of mind." Meanwhile we are all makeshifts, and the better people are, the worse misfit. "He that departeth from evil maketh himself a prey." Nevertheless we cannot escape the challenge of Paul, "Be not conformed to this age!" We may be confident, however, that "the fashion of this age passes away."

> Our little systems have their day;
> They have their day and cease to be;
> They are but broken lights of thee;
> And thou, O Lord, art more than they.

16

THE SCIENCE OF LIFE

IN RESPECT to the organization of life itself, biology far transcends the old botany and zoology with their emphasis on mere classification. The attempt to arrive at a comprehensive grasp of phenomena by perfect classification is indeed futile, for no sooner do we attain a satisfactory classification than something turns up to upset it, so that we have to start over.

Furthermore, to go very far with a class theory is likely to be fallacious, inasmuch as we cannot know enough about a class in general to predict the behavior of class members under diverse circumstances. Phenomena are better studied in terms of the field where they occur and of the forces impinging at the point than on the plausible but superficial basis of classification, which leads us to say, "Dogs are faithful" or "Chinese are tricky."

Consequently, when we want to control the conditions of life, we need to know something more than life forms and how they are to be classified. It is far more important to know the operative factors in the various situations. Even in popular speech, not all mushrooms are toadstools, and not all "germs" are enemies. Some dogs may be intrinsically wolves, yet not merely safe but serviceable. Not all communists are Stalinists, and not all Catholics are "jesuitical" (whatever that may mean). Generalization is necessary, but highly dangerous.

THE SCIENCE OF LIFE

Thus while man is unavoidably classed as an animal, it is necessary to make discriminating use of the information; hence the role of biology, which reminds us that we "are all of the earth earthy" but at the same times gives us a basis for understanding our place in nature. The present generation is greatly in need of a current equivalent of Drummond's <u>Ascent</u> <u>of</u> <u>Man</u>, which two generations ago poeticized the unfolding of the biological potential for conscience and culture.

Biology does indeed put meaning into the reminder that we are all animals, which was to Paul the core of the moral struggle. We must carefully avoid, however, the application to the "lower" creations of projections of human experience. Animals are not "cruel," "bestial," "brutish"; for such epithets apply only to potentially rational self-conscious beings that behave as if they were not rational persons. The present revolt against "living rationally" may have a color of justification in the fact that no one is chiefly, or even highly, rational, but it does not follow that the normal preponderance of impulse, emotion, sentiment warrants us in living irrationally, in defiance of reason.

For we are not mere animals, and human biology must be studied in the light of psychology and sociology — just as must indeed animal biology itself, for animals develop on a basis of mind and society. Indeed the study of animal society and animal behavior is a prerequisite to full mastery of our social sciences. There was a time, to be sure, when scholarship went off at a tangent and applied to man all that had been worked out on the subject of "instinct." Trotter's Instinct of the Herd in Peace and in War had a notable influence on thought thirty years ago, as did McDougall's Social Psychology with its array of "instincts." Now, however, we know that the concept of instinct as mechanism is baseless, and that animal behavior is not piecemeal but integral. We know also that the term "instinct" is devoid of scientific meaning in any field. It begs the whole question and explains nothing. Thus what was once regarded as a great biological contribution to psychology and sociology is now seen to be completely sterile.

Biology can, nonetheless, challenge us with the problem of holding our own in the life scheme. It appears, indeed, that mankind may be yielding to the insects. Man is even hastening his own doom by the very weapons he uses against the insects. He poisons the soil with lead and arsenic sprays and kills the earthworms that keep the earth from compacting and smothering the roots. He distributes on fruits and vegetables metallic spray residues that are subjecting whole populations to cumulative lead and arsenic poisoning. He fills the air of cities and the dust of highways with similar poison, to be sure, because of an engineering fad that has misled him about motor efficiency, but this mania cannot be charged to biology as can the fad for spraying with DDT, with resultant cumulative poisoning of cattle, butter fat, and human livers. Very likely such battles against insect pests do more harm than do the pests themselves.

Properly understood and used, however, biology

could put us in command of the organic basis of mind, morals, and socialization. The glandular psychology, in particular, explains more of human ways than would have been thought possible in the days when man was homo sapiens. Here, however, caution is necessary, for much glandular malfunctioning is not a primary cause, but rather a result of bad thinking and evil social situations. To sever nerves carrying damaging impulses is a sorry substitute for the integration of personality and the regeneration of society. Likewise in the higher realms of neural process. Cerebral surgery for "the amputation of conscience" is a paltry makeshift in a world of overpowering social maladjustment. The current doping with sedatives or stimulants begets no safety for the soul. The new psychosomatic medicine with its attempt at integral treatment of personality is more promising than the old quackery, but it will be invalid unless it takes fully into account the social conditioning of body, mind, and personality.

Biology perhaps better than any other science can reinforce the meaning of the organismic as against the mechanistic pattern. Mechanistic schematizations have, to be sure, been used in the attempt to make animal function more comprehensible to machine-minded students. The brain is the office, the heart the engine-room. Blood vessels are the pipes and tubes that keep a modern edifice functioning. Nerves are the telephone and light wires; and so on. Comprehension so gained is, however, scrappy and delusive, and does more harm than good; for in the case of gregarious animals it is primarily the group that behaves, and in any case it is the organism as a whole. Even in the subtler reaches of life, it is apparent that tissues develop according to their location in the organic whole, and heredity is not a mechanistic problem of summating distinct determiners inasmuch as each gene functions as a phase of the whole chromosomic pattern, and not in isolation. Neither can we hold any longer to Weissmann's insulation of the germ plasm, inasmuch as we know it to be accessible to chemical and physical influences creative of heritable mutations. Life is "all of a piece," just as the universe is all of a piece.

Biology as written is still too largely mechanistic under the spell of an engineering technology. We are on the verge, however, of a new biologic era with food from the sea or from rapid multiplication of yeasts, or from cereals bred to yield sugar direct instead of starch, giving immunity to arctic temperatures. Such trends, lifting achievement above the purely mechanical and undermining the spell of mechanism with its agelong hypnotic influence on human thought and action, will make biology more highly serviceable to general understanding

17

THE USE OF CHEMISTRY

AS WITH other sciences, chemistry has until now filled mostly a mechanistic role, with little regard to universals and ultimates. Benzoate of soda was made available as a disguise for food improperly prepared. Agene yielded ghastly whiteness to bread while deteriorating the product. Sulphur dioxide was used to bleach fruits — and destroy white blood corpuscles. The inventor of DDT received a huge prize for enabling us to add to our foods a cumulative poison. Lead was added to gasoline as an engineering trick, and wood alcohol in the radiator augmented the hazards. Everything has been done for some person's momentary advantage, without regard to general or long-run considerations.

Such a situation is natural in the hit-or-miss social order to which we cling. Beyond that, it goes with the fragmentary state from which chemistry has not entirely escaped. Within a generation, however, chemistry, by the discovery of new elements, has closed most of its gaps and is perhaps in sight of the time when any conceivable reaction can be known in advance, its equation coming as precisely as any mathematical formulation, simply because when all the gaps in the periodic system are closed everything hangs together with everything else and chemistry becomes mathematics.

Thus chemistry reinforces the idea that this is a universe without gaps. When half the elements remained undiscovered, the piecemeal state of the science was not favorable to an integral view of things, but now, through physical chemistry and bio-chemistry, the science is ready to reach out and cover all realms, so that we get the conception of a chemical universe in which there are no intractable areas.

We are impressed at the same time with the unavoidability of causality. An element of mystery remains until such time as all reactions can be mathematically predicted, and the psychology of the situation has a tinge of acceptance of "chance," even though the scientist would repudiate such conceptions. The sense of interrelation and interdependence is, however, becoming more clearcut, and possible room for causeless occurrence shrinks. Not that there is a mechanistic pattern, as is commonly supposed, but that the results of any whole situation, including not merely substances but environing conditions, are precisely predetermined. The chemical equation may record only a special part of the story but the whole, with inclusion of such aspects as temperature, pressure, catalyzer, and the like, could be put in an unmistakable formula, so that the correlation with things in general would leave no room for uncertainty. That situation is what we call "causation."

By such steps, chemistry leads toward an understanding of even the process of life. As long as we think in mechanistic terms, life will be elusive, for it is always a quality of an integral situation. Certainly t cannot be pieced together by mere chemical synthesis, nor can it be understood by mere analysis. Even now, however, biochemistry points toward integral conceptions of the wholeness we call life. We know how much depends on the chemistry of the organism, and how that relates to the life situation as a whole. To date, undue emphasis has been put on chemical intervention in the treatment of disease. Osteopaths and chiropractors have extended our conceptions of the capacities of the organism in adjustment, but have perhaps overstressed merely mechanical adjustment. Now psychosomatic medicine is getting ready to put mere chemistry and physics in due subordination to the general life scheme. The patient will cease to expect miracles from medication or from mechanical realinement and will be induced to seek wholeness of personality, as religious leaders have verbally insisted must be done, though with little facility for furthering the process. The chemical treatment of disease will then fall into its proper place as a momentary crutch instead of being a naive reliance as it is at present for the generality of people, who are offended when a doctor does not give something out of a bottle. The psychological technique already utilized by osteopaths or chiropractors will balance merely bodily adjustments in a scientific fashion until the person is whole," that is, well.

Chemistry can, however, throw light on the workings of personality itself. The ancients were moving toward a chemistry of behavior, as when they named "melancholy," that is, "black bile," but we can find a

chemical explanation for deviations of conduct, and w
are becoming slower to attribute misconduct to mer
wilfulness or malice. Of course glandular therapy is no
final, inasmuch as the malfunctioning of glands ma
be caused by disorders of personality, in which cas
chemical treatment is but a makeshift. If, however, th
chemical manifestations are treated as symptoms, no
to be suppressed but to be traced back to their sourc
they may yield clear clues in personality problems. Thu:
for instance, the erratic sex behavior of elderly men ma'
betoken not sin as such, but the decline of glandular se
cretion, and the necessity of readjustment of personalit'
patterns. Chemistry will not abolish sin, but it ma'
enable such an understanding of specific sins as wil
facilitate more wholesome living.

In an all-round way, indeed, chemistry can continu
man's effort to master the universe. If once we get a1
over-all conception of the problem of society and natur(
so that chemistry, instead of claiming mastery, fall
into due subordination to the inclusive pattern, we shal
be on our way to the control now so desperately needec

Chemistry can never do its perfect work as less tha1
a general social project looking to the permanent benefi
of all concerned. The lure of momentary profit for pro
moters cannot be made a safe standard of procedure. In
novations must be withheld until their remotest reache
have been checked from the standpoint of health an
safety. Thus immediate damage and costly retracing o
steps may be averted and net progress accelerated

Moreover the products of chemical progress must b

made immediately available at minimum prices. The profits for financing industry should be drawn from well-established luxury goods and not from the advancing frontier of common needs. There is probably no reason, for instance, why a large proportion of drugs should not be made as cheap as cocoa or cinnamon.

As important, however, as the direct material benefit from the new chemistry will be the impetus to general understanding when chemistry ceases to be looked upon by the public as magic or sorcery and becomes a familiar and intimate part of the everyday texture of common thought, so that the whole scheme of things will be looked upon as a dynamic continuity holding experience together on the basis of causal certainty, without breach or gap. The Christian is of course reminded of Him in whom "all things hold together."

18

THE USE OF PHYSICS

NOW that nineteenth century materialism with its deifi
cation of stuff has faded away, not merely chemistry
but also physics is ready for an interpretation tha
reaches over into the realms traditionally designated a
spiritual. Scientists are not concerned over denials tha
"matter" exists, inasmuch as what appears to the sense:
as stuff turns out to be energy and motion, and abou
all that appears in last analysis is a mathematica
formula, which, however, serves the purpose that "matter" used to serve.

Wordsworth long ago expressed a conception of
spiritual reality that answers word for word to modern
conceptions of matter:

> And I have felt
> A presence that disturbs me with the joy
> Of elevated thoughts: a sense sublime
> Of something far more deeply interfused,
> Whose dwelling is the light of setting suns,
> And the round ocean and the living air
> And the blue sky, and in the mind of man:
> A motion and a spirit, that impels
> All thinking things, all objects of all thought,
> And rolls through all things.

Certainly physics suggests that matter is organismic,
not mechanistic, and the understanding of it is not a

uestion of summating electrons, protons, neutrons, and
hat not, but of detecting the overruling pattern that
ives all of them their meaning, their nature, their
ery existence. For none of the items into which sub-
tance can be dissected has any reality save as a detail
n an integral pattern, just as the dots in a stipple pic-
ure have significance only according to their distribu-
ion in varying dispersion and density, which consti-
ites the picture.

The new physics raises, however, new issues about
ausality and freedom. Because there are certain aspects
f the internal processes of matter that cannot at present
e measured, some scientists have talked about "indeter-
inacy," as if some occurrences were uncaused. Moreover
ie lack of identicalness among atoms and electrons of
ie same substance raises questions of "individuality"
iat call for statistical determination to replace old
inceptions of identicalness of particles, and thereby a
eming uncertainty replaces the old fixity. Nothing has
een said, however, to lead to the supposition that any-
iing can happen for no reason. The "freedom" that
insists in the fact that occurrences are not, or maybe
ever can be, measured is obviously not objective free-
om but merely freedom from man's observation, which
of course an irrelevancy so far as the essence of things
concerned. Once more we face the fact that man's
iinking is anthropomorphic, anthropocentric, but it
oes not follow that what he can know is all that there
to know, or ever will be. Certainly the new physics
oes not rule out determinacy or enthrone freedom in the

street-corner sense of the term. There are still reasons fo
everything, whether we can grasp them or not.

If such were not the case we could not view physic
as so promising an instrument for the control of th
universe as it now seems to be. If in final analysis ther
is but one substance, or rather but one energy, it woul
seem that we are approaching the time when we can d
whatever we please with anything — when we shall b
relatively independent of traditional resources. Just a
chemistry in the plastic age enables us to make anythin
out of anything, so physics points through atomic re
search to the harnessing of prime creativity — except, o
course, that the outcome depends entirely on our com
mand of the all-embracing pattern. We are back t
Plato's conception that nothing is real save the idea i
the mind of God, and all our centuries of improvisatior
patchwork, piecemeal contrivance, have proven to us tha
whereas mechanistic procedure tends to ultimate destruc
tion and chaos, the possibility still remains of thinkin
integrally, organismically, in order to head off disin
tegration and chaos.

The atomic scientists themselves have arrived at th
notion that all science is social science. Their efforts to b
delivered from the consequences of their own ingenuit
register the folly of a purely mechanistic approach i
research. Only science expressive of the integral interest
of humanity as a whole is tenable or tolerabl

19

SCIENCE AND ART

RELIGION and science are both social approaches to the universe, different phases of the central human interest, and a survey of the history of art shows that the aesthetic interest covers the same ground and points in the same direction, so that goodness, truth, and beauty coincide. If we are to love the Lord our God with all our minds, we are also to worship the Lord in the beauty of holiness.

There is indeed no sharp distinction between science and art. The argument that science is cumulative whereas art was as great centuries ago as it is now, if not greater, quite misses the point. For one thing, it is doubtful whether the profuse science of today is actually putting us more in command of safety, security, and the good life than did science in ancient Greece. In fact it may well be argued that the only science that matters is that which is effectively applied in man's interest, and that the present generation is more at a loss than any other has ever been; simply for the reason that we are putting into effective use a continually smaller and smaller proportion of available knowledge. Very likely it is only in an abstract intellectual sense, an academic sense, that science is cumulative, for the pragmatic test is in the development of personality and the safety of the soul.

Furthermore, it is only by abstract and arbitrarily artificial standards that the art of one period can be

117

declared equal or superior to that of a quite different period. Surely the facilities of structural metal, plastics and all the technical discoveries of recent years make possible the same cumulative "progress" in the arts as science is alleged to manifest. It might even be argued that the Empire State Building is finer art than the Great Pyramid or the Parthenon by reason of the superior facilities available and employed. In any case there can be no absolute standard; the major part of any criterion must be relevant to time and place and circumstance.

That art and science are not sharply distinguishable is apparent from the fact that a good artist is master of the relevant science and a good scientist is artistic in method and appreciation. The would-be musician bent only on performance and impatient of theory will never be an artist, for his technique will be amateurish and makeshift. On the other hand there is something lacking in the scientist who is sloppy and slovenly and who has no eye for the aesthetic aspect of his achievement. A good surgeon appreciates "a beautiful cancer."

Much in point is Darwin's testimony that the atrophy of his original literary and aesthetic interests had not merely stunted his personality but possibly lowered his intellectual efficiency. He was positive that if he had his life to live over he would cherish his "finer" sensibilities.

The development of art, like that of science, is of course a function of man's social experience. The basis of art rests, to be sure, in the rhythm of organic functioning but the actual patterns assumed in the course of art history express directly or symbolize the values arrived at by the group in its struggle for existence and wellbeing. W. Flinders Petrie's <u>Revolutions of Civilization</u> offers graphic evidence of the manner in which the quality of art mirrors the vicissitudes of culture from incipience to climax and decadence. The initiated can tell by the forms of art what stage in the culture cycle they represent.

A very pertinent illustration is found in the bizarre developments of cubism and futurism before the first World War, which so resembled the chaos of stage scene-shifting that it was possible at that time to interpret them as expressive of the confusion attendant on the end of an epoch. Very shortly came the European crash which verified the interpretation. Aesthetics had been, perhaps, a better key than economics and politics to the collapse of a culture.

People in general, however, have not learned to accept so close a correlation. Many critics still try to treat art as if it existed in a vacuum and show umbrage if anyone insists that art has no meaning save in its social correlations. It is no wonder, then, that the layman still builds Gothic churches on Kansas prairies, in blissful ignorance of the fact that architecture must express the surrounding culture, not to speak of employing the media of the locale as Ruskin so urgently required. Obviously, Gothic cathedrals are as misplaced on the Great Plains as date palms or papaya trees would be, and they no more express prairie culture than would palmetto structures thatched with tropical foliage, but the cult of the esthete delays recognition of such essentials of value.

THE CULTURAL CONCEPT OF CHRISTIANITY

Obviously art would, under such conditions, profit from explicit union with science, natural and social, just as would science from a realization that science that eventuates in ugliness is an abortion. Our industrial cities have long professed devotion to music and art but their delay in clearing their atmospheres belies their professions. The sordid qualities of a mercenary culture yield both a science and an art low in human values. Particularly is the immuring of art in virtual storage to be scanned ignorantly by gaping sight-seers entirely unaware of meanings and implications, a betrayal of the general emptiness of a culture whose everyday life is only beginning to be tinged with beauty. Certainly the world has never had any quota of specialized art save on a basis of parasitism, and art will never be genuinely honorable till it is a pervasive spontaneous expression of the common life, just as in the simplest tribal culture.

The diffusion of artistic ability and aesthetic experience is indeed a test of the validity of scientific experience, spiritual insight, and general culture. When laboratories and factories have the charm of cathedrals, when cathedrals fit their settings and their congregations, and when the pattern of a culture partakes of epic and lyric charm, we can at least believe in measurable progress. Such conditions will not, however, be reached till we assume that every person has it in him to be the creator of art, as well as to advance in some degree the sum total of human knowledge, and to experience and communicate distinctive spiritual values.

Apart from a general social regeneration, the first

step toward such an integral consummation is for adults to let children draw and paint and make music as seems good to children instead of shaming or coaxing them into turning out what adults approve when it comes from adults. The present practice thwarts the normal development and kills art possibilities. Furthermore, just as in religion and science, unless the grown-ups become as little children they cannot enter the kingdom. As Goethe learned from Herder, true art is appreciated by ordinary people not specially trained in appreciation. On the other hand, much so-called art appreciation in sophisticated circles is admiration for technique, which has nothing to do with aesthetics proper. So far are we from a wholesome sense of social values.

The general neglect of the social sciences, or their perversion into pettifogging, accounts for much of the cultural dislocation that persists. The development of courses, however, in the sociology of art, the sociology of science, the sociology of religion, will exhibit the correlation existing among these several fields and will hasten the amalgamation of the true, the beautiful, and the good. Then neither art nor science nor religion will plume itself on isolation and self-sufficiency, but each will find its meaning in the others and in integration with the general scheme of our collective life.

20

ART, SCIENCE, AND PERSONALITY

IF, AS BERGSON SAYS, the distinctive achievement of intellect is the making of tools, especially tools for the fashioning of other tools, and of infinitely varying their manufacture, then surely science and art set their zeal on mental attainment, for they are surely tools par excellence, not merely for technological purposes, but also for the elaboration of personality, character, and faith.

Science and art do, indeed, differentiate us notably from mere clods and worms, which possess, to be sure, a certain beauty and a certain skill creatively imparted to them, but not the ability to multiply their own skill and their own charm, whereas man in the ordinary course of life has manifested the ability to do both. He has often, it may well be admitted, perverted his faculties toward stupidity, incompetence, waste, and ugliness, but nevertheless the potentialities are manifest in the direction of higher things, and mankind may well arrive even yet in spite of the waste of material, energy, and personality in unconscionable fumbling.

Science and art undergird and reinforce spiritual experience, which may, indeed, be in itself spontaneous, but which certainly requires direction and nurture if it is to be more than an abortion. Those that have nothing to show for their lives but the "wood, hay, stubble" that Paul laments testify mightily to the insufficiency of mere right-heartedness. Unless, indeed, the vital spark be quickened and intensified, informed with intelligence, beauty, and power, even salvation becomes a haunting tragedy. Religion cannot thrive without science and art.

It needs organismic science as the intellectual evidence for Christianity, as the unfolding of experience into a broadening and deepening sense of the wholeness of things, the wholeness of life, the integrity of spirit, which identifies insight, logic, reason, sanity with the meaning embodied in and revealed through the fulness and the wholeness of Christ. It needs, also, integral art, as a direct testimony and a direct incentive to the growth and blossoming of the transformed personality "from Glory to Glory, even as by the Lord, the Spirit." Certainly Christianity has no room for stupidity, obscurantism, meretriciousness, or ugliness.

Unfortunately both mechanistic science and vacuous art have been entirely capable of subverting the foundations of life. A generation brought up on the idea that everything is piecemeal, that learning consists in accumulating mere information and petty skills, that everything can be blue-printed and pigeonholed, that art is a thing in itself, that standards of criticism exist in a vacuum, and that art is exalted by aloofness is in no position to take life seriously and to live it deeply. Such fatuities must be entirely superseded before a bona-fide Christianity can blossom and thrive.

When, however, science and art manifest themselves as integral and reciprocal ventures on a basis of vital faith in the wholeness of creation and the soundness of experience, then they give concrete substance to what might otherwise remain ethereal and fanciful, or even illusory, and they become direct and immediate evidence for Christianity. They talk, indeed, a universal language that vivifies the traditional theology and vivifies its symbolizations, giving present worth and meaning to what might otherwise be mere verbalization.

Thus, for instance, the atonement, which evangelicals are wont to couch in a forbidding formula borrowed from the law courts and the class in mathematics, becomes an artistic and valid expression of the principle of social integration, personal identification, and collective salvation, all of which are essential to health, soundness, and persistence of personality.

Thus science and art contribute to the basic and ultimate mastery of life, not merely in terms of day to day interests, needs, and fulfillments, but in respect to our ability to "rise on stepping stones" of our "dead selves to higher things." In proportion as the right hearted man loves the Lord "with all his mind," he avails himself of all the resources of science for the deliverance of the race from scarcity and constraint. In proportion as he loves the Lord "with all his heart" he enlists all the possibilities of figure, symbolism, grace and beauty in behalf of a world free from baldness, bareness, flatness, and ugliness, so that this planet may answer to our imaginings of heaven. Thus science and art attain their consummation in the fulfillment of faith.

It has been the custom of devotees to treat science, art, and religion pretty much as ends in themselves and to forget the human consequences, but an integral view of the inclusive realm makes it apparent that all values in whatever sphere consist solely in contribution to personality. All real attainments, indeed, eventuate in personality as the measure of all experience and all value. Thus however much a candid scientific analysis may seem at first glimpse to discount personality and to swallow up the individual in the cosmic process and the social whole, it turns out that this integration magnifies the meaning of personality and the worth of the individual as the only measure of whether anything is worth while. Certainly nothing has any meaning or worth save as it ministers to the exaltation of individuality and personality, not in detachment and isolation but as vital nuclei and foci of the social process.

Science and art are thus, in terms of both faith and achievement, facets of the integral evidence for Christianity, which is attested by our aspirations no less than by our attainments. They both point in the direction indicated by Christ in his challenge to be perfect as our father in heaven is perfect.

21

INTEGRAL EDUCATION

IF IT BE ASSUMED that education is a means toward general integration of society and personality, then education must be sharply distinguished from vocational training and from departmentalism, both of which lead to partial, fragmentary, and abortive results save in so far as they are completely subordinated to general culture. Particularly does a Christian emphasis arrive at this conclusion about the educational process, for nothing fragmentary is Christian.

The only justification, indeed, for the maintenance of schools and colleges under Christian auspices lies in the fact that it is a Christian duty to master knowledge and skill as an integral whole basic to the conquest of life in behalf of comprehensive human interest. The traditional Christian emphasis on "liberal arts" education represents a fairly consistent effort in this direction, however limited the outlook and however faulty the results. Particularly must "an educated ministry" be vastly broader than vocational or professional training can provide, and the same is true of all other walks of life in a society aspiring to be Christian.

The so-called essentialists now in revolt against "progressive education" are squinting in the wrong direction. It is indeed true that most present-day schools fail to impart effectively the rudiments of education,

ut no amount of engraining of elementary skills, how-
ver inclusive, can yield an educated personality. As
ong as the present bungling social order and the present
orm of individualism are taken as standard, there can
e no effective integration of either personality or society.

As far as pedagogical technique goes, "progressive
ducation" was pointed aright, but it has been at fault in
ocusing unduly on the individual, as if wholesome
ersonality could be achieved in an unwholesome society.
Our social order is so much worse than the general dis-
positions and potentialities of its participants, solely
because it has been allowed to develop at random, without systematic consideration and orderly planning, that
it cannot be taken as a standard or as a setting for integral personalities. It is a thankless task to try to produce much Christian character in a pagan society. A
few heroic individuals may become notably superior to
the current norm, but usually at the cost of such strain
and tension as to favor neuroses.

Adequate education, then, will go beyond both
"essentialism" and "progressism" in that its prime purpose will be to fashion a new social order on the
principle, "Be not conformed to this age, for the fashion
of this age passes away." Such is indeed the lesson of
history, inadequately presented, to be sure, in the usual
histories of education, as also in the ordinary histories
of society and culture.

It follows, of course, that no group, no community devoted to the preservation of tradition and the
entrenchment of vested interests can really promote

education, as contrasted with training. The present at
tempt to subordinate education to the maintenance o:
"the democratic way of life" is a case in point, for historically democracy has been a device for enlisting th
masses in behalf of the control of life by the busines:
interests. So effective has this subterfuge been that th
very term "democracy" is permanently spoiled for use a:
an instrument of social progress.

There is even fear that the same may be true of
"Christianity," simply because so many publicizers apply the term "Christian" promiscuously as a device for
lending sanction to dubious projects, as if there were
"Christian nations" or as if "Christendom" were not
essentially pagan. If the word "Christian" is to be sal-
vaged for legitimate use there will have to be rapid action for the Christianization of the social order.

Integral education will, indeed, start with such an
assumption. It will ignore vested interests of every sort.
It will abandon all values less than the common welfare of all mankind. Thus it cannot sanction any lesser
loyalties, but must shape everything in terms of equal
consideration for the possibilities of all branches of the
human race and equal devotion to the welfare of all
persons present and future. Neither science nor Christianity lends any color of support to any sort of provincialism or particularism or traditionalism.

If then a community can be found to sponsor real
education, the first principle will be universality and
integration. The student will be regarded as a focus of
social forces, a resultant personality to be oriented to

ocial change. The smallest child will be recognized s a spontaneous individual whose mind is to be appealed to on a basis of give-and-take equality. His thought and performance will be respected and encouraged in terms of its own interest and its own competence, and sophisticated adult standards will not be inflicted. It will be found, indeed, that save for need of more information and more experience his reasoning s on the same basis as that of adults, but his unspoiled astes and preferences are sounder than the choices of the dult, and if he is given a chance he will arrive at alues superior to those of present-day adults. Parents nd teachers must, accordingly, be willing to have heir values transcended and outmoded as the new generation moves into a more human world.

Unless, however, groups can be found to practise he necessary self-abnegation, the necessary repudiation f traditional values, the necessary conformity to a eckoning future, society will continue mired in pagan onvention and blind conformity to the patterns that ave ruined the world. "The American Way of Life" s too mechanical, too incoherent, too unreasoning, too ompetitive, too predatory, too wasteful, to furnish a nodel for an integral culture, a Christian world order.

Looking, however, toward a new education we are n process of subordinating departmentalism to the requirements of general culture. We are beginning to develop teachers with insight and far-reaching competence, ot in "subjects" but in society and personality. We are learning that "telling is not teaching" and that lecturing must make way for the give and take of group discussion. We are shaping a curriculum, indeed, pointed to the world's needs. The danger is, however, that these hopeful trends will be enmeshed in a new propaganda, a new formalism, and perverted into tools for a new world conflict of ideologies and systems. It is not yet apparent whether education can indeed educate instead of remaining a tool of vested interests to perpetuate the circle of their privilege.

22

INTEGRAL SOCIETY

FROM the drift of the foregoing argument it is apparent
that proper integration of personality depends upon proper integration of society, which can no longer be on less
than a world scale. Either we attain "one world," or everything is abortive.

It should be clear, however, that the newborn child
cannot be directly assimilated to a world community, to
the great society, for the gap is too vast. Hence there
must intervene a smaller, more intimate community as
mediator between the individual personality and human-
ty at large.

The old-fashioned homogeneous neighborhood used
to be capable of negotiating this problem, for it could
easily assimilate the child and imperceptibly, almost,
naturalize him in the great world as that used to be
when the great world was no more than a region, or in
a shadowy way a small nation. Now, however, the
extremes are so very remote, and the local community
has become so tenuous that rarely if ever does the adjustment of the newborn occur as a matter of course, and
usually it does not take place passably at all. Most
people are adrift in a cosmic society too vast to be
comprehended or even imagined.

In some instances an interest group has been more
effective than the neighborhood. Some of the small

religious denominations, for instance, have been an ef
fective step beyond the family and have effectively toppe
off the child's personality through a sense of membershi
in "the little flock" or in "the Kingdom of God," destine
to inherit the earth. Even when such a group, as for in
stance, Jehovah's Witnesses, becomes multitudinous, it
assimilative power and its conquering ardor may for
time remain adequate. The individual is not conforme
to this age, but to an age ahead. He is thus rather ef
fectively socialized and humanized and developed int
a tolerable personality.

Such a socializing agency is, however, somethin
short of universal, and integration cannot be complet
Indeed the strains and tensions engendered by confli
with "the world" may threaten the integrity of the pe
sonality itself. Unless the provisional fellowship
really capable of expanding to include all mankind,
falls short of being an adequate agency of integratio

To many the labor movement has seemed capab
of becoming an all-inclusive locus of integration an
loyalty, simply because it is perhaps the one function
grouping open to all mankind. Certainly as long as w
are in an age of deficit wrestling with scarcity, it woul
seem that a fellowship of all so engaged must hav
vital and dynamic possibilities of an all-embracin
sort. If all actual producers could awake to their con
mon interest and pool their energies the results would b
incalculable and the ensuing solidarity would spell in
tegration for all persons and for the world orde

Unfortunately, however, too many are concerne

more with beating the game than with focusing all human energies; so while for many "the union" is the compelling focus of loyalty, the socializer of the new generation, it is almost impossible for labor in any land to get even a clear majority of the population, even when the working farmers become labor conscious, especially as the success of the movement begets new circles of power and privilege more concerned with prerogative in the present system than with a world community of those that toil. It even seems impossible to consolidate an effective world federation of unions, not to speak of a political international.

Some have thought of the church as the effective mediator of socialization and integration, but sectarianism and internecine conflict, such as that between modernism and fundamentalism, have so far made it impossible to achieve any effective unity on even a national basis except by the betrayal of Christianity. As far as appears, moreover, Christendom is no more competently adjusted to the present world crisis than is the non-Christian world.

Many persons in many lands are sure that the Rochdale co-operative movement is the key to ultimate human unity. Its basis in personality and equality would indeed seem to give it the primary requisites for effective integration, and it is more successfully international than most other organized movements. Certainly it is one effective nursery of wholesome personality, of neighborhood mutuality, of national and international

133

reciprocity, and its structure may well become a key section of a new world order. As yet, however, it has not escaped the trammels of a business psychology, and effective membership participation is rather fragmentary and sporadic. How far the movement's identification with Christian purposes and labor strategy may enhance its binding power is not yet certain.

A few enthusiasts cherish hopes for the regeneration and revitalization of the small community in the historic sense. Most of the human race have been villagers, dominated by locale, and to some degree it has proved possible to reconstitute the neighborhood, even within sizeable cities. The general problem seems, however, to have got out of hand. Even a place of two thousand inhabitants, while not too large to be possessed of a community psychology, is likely to be essentially a city, where neighbors may sicken, die, and be buried without any general awareness. In the United States, particularly, bigness is so worshipped that no heed is paid to the mandate, "Despise not the day of small things." How to reverse the tide and revive the integral small community, while easy to demonstrate logically in economic and social terms, is not so easy to accomplish by way of a revolution in social psychology. If the decentralists have the answer, it will tax their utmost ingenuity to make it operative.

If Christianity is to have any part in the recovery of integrality, it will, of course, have to interpret its mandates in terms of all the sciences and all the arts. It is not sufficient to comfort or to enliven the individual.

INTEGRAL SOCIETY

There must be a convincing pattern for the economic system, for the political system, for the social order, all finding their meaning in the functional enlargement of personality. Certainly Christianity is capable of identification with all that is constructive in all the movements indicated, and if its potential can be released and focused the problem is as good as solved.

At present, however, Christianity lingers in the realm of abstract piety and verbal pronouncement or even is subverted to the purposes of the pagan state. The church has not striven to set the authority of Christ over worldly statecraft, but has ordinarily acquiesced in the most tragic enormities of a godless and inhuman diplomacy. In view of what is known about the power of a determined minority it cannot be doubted that the genuine Christians could shape the ruling policies of the world did they once set their hearts and their minds on the task, but they prefer to take opposing sides on major issues and to cancel one another out. The "greater works" that Jesus commissioned us to do are but meagerly in evidence.

In consequence, Christians in general seem subject to the same neuroses as are other citizens, and they will continue to be so as long as it is conventional to profess one pattern of life but to tolerate the organization of society on a quite opposite pattern. Indeed a very intense devotion to Christianity is devastating unless it is effectively implemented by a continual struggle to make Christ's principles prevail in every sphere of life. Efforts at proper behavior in face-to-face relations will

135

not save the sanity of the person that ignores the claims of Christ on the collective choices that in an impersonal way govern the world. The divided conscience, the split personality, are not fruits of Christianity.

From such a predicament we cannot be delivered by abstractions. It will be necessary to discover how to put all earth's resources at the equal disposal of every human need and how to make all mankind cheerfully co-operative for the solution of every human problem. It is easy to demonstrate in theory that such mutuality would greatly enhance every sane personality and go far to prevent neurosis. Because, however, man is but slightly rational, the appeal to reason is only moderately effective and of itself contains small incentive to action. The potentiality of man for mutual aid has, however, been an enormous factor in the struggle for existence. It has, indeed, served as a mainspring of history. Spiritually enlivened by the evangel of Jesus it is capable of serving as the key to world unity, human integration, and the unfolding of wholesome personality.

23

THE ECONOMIC PATTERN

INASMUCH as we are all of the earth earthy, all our projects are so dependent on the "material" wherewithal that the amount and quality thereof substantially determines what purposes, what ideals, we will in fact seriously formulate. Schemes transcending such tangible means fall in the category of wishful thinking. They may indeed result ultimately in new discoveries and inventions that will make them feasible, but meanwhile we remain anchored to the solid earth.

This is why, for one thing, every population undergoing modern technological development begins at a certain stage to limit deliberately its rate of increase. Such limitation has, however, been mostly on a narrow and selfish basis uncorrelated with the actual optimum for maximum economic and social development. The planning of an integral society will involve, however, a proper calculation as to the most effective ratio between population and resources and will work for its attainment in practice. We are not commanded to overfill the earth and to swamp it.

Granting an approximation to a workable population ratio, it will be necessary, of course, to "subdue" the earth in terms of a balanced conservation and utilization of resources so that without stinting any generation the productivity of the earth may be permanently maintained and enhanced. Before the release of atomic energy, it was hard to see how such an ideal could be consistently maintained and approximated, but now there is no problem save the human problem of making man willing to save mankind.

The resources made available and conserved by a free play of science and technology released by the abandonment of provincial, nationalistic, or other subhuman restrictions must, of course, be at the equal disposal of all the people of the world. The spread of enlightenment will introduce population limitation in consonance with canons of expediency, so that we can get beyond the danger of having the more fortunate areas overwhelmed by the surplus multiplication of backward areas. Once such an equilibrium is struck, there can be no tenable excuse for any monopolistic withholding of resources on any pretext of social policy.

Within any community, region, nation, or continent, moreover, it will be necessary to provide explicitly for the equal access of all people to the full possibilities of the good life. There can be no justification for letting poverty limit any individual or any group in its effort to measure up to maximum possibilities of education, training, productivity, and general culture. The complete basic welfare of the entire population will be a matter-of-course foundation principle of public policy. Expansion will be financed by taking toll of luxury and not by a levy on the essentials of life, which will be made available in abundance without question.

Moreover the economic system will have to become

not merely self-governing but governed by the collective initiative of its participants. A wholesome social order will not be satisfied with meeting consumer needs, or even with the maintenance of proper conditions of work, but will ordain that the realm of production shall be a laboratory of personality and society where the population may learn not merely self-discipline but also the processes of controlling and administering the common interests. Government of the workers, by the workers, for the workers is just as opposite to the industrial and administrative situation in economics as is the cognate principle in the realm of civic affairs. Government from the top down is irreconcilable with the free development of personality. An enlightened population would be willing, if necessary, to sacrifice some efficiency in order to be completely self-governing, in the economic as in other realms.

Obviously, too, there will be a planned economy based on advance measurement of trends and needs. The economic system cannot be allowed to move by fits and starts in frantic curves of up and down. The element of chance will be made negligible by spreading all risks over the whole world system, so that they can be carried without shock and spasm. Individuals and groups will not be free to gamble with resources or to operate in the economic sphere according to mere taste and whim. If adventure is still craved it can be sought in Nature and in sport, but certainly not where the interests of others are at stake.

The economic system will be a laboratory for the

educational system, just as it was in the days of house
hold industry, when all learning was vitalized by it
association with doing. Instead of excluding children
from industry, a wise society will give them the satis
faction of being early useful, and their product will go
a long way toward financing education. No longe
will there be an academic realm, where people lear
what they have no intention of living by.

We shall arrive, in fact, at the time when th
economic system will be required to deliver not merely
the necessary commodities but also the possibilities of
real education and of enlivening and ennobling occupation. Certainly no economic system can be considered
tolerable however much stuff it may turn out unless i
provides the whole population with gratifying and in-
spiring occupation as the nucleus of the good life. Until
production becomes at least as gratifying personally to
the workers as does the consumption of the product we
cannot consider that we have a tenable economic system

People used to wonder who in a proper economic
system would "do the dirty work." Technology, however, makes it apparent that there is no reason why there
should be any appreciable amount of dangerous, un-
healthy, or filthy occupation. The street-sweeper of today
can wear as immaculate clothing as does the limousine
chauffeur and contact dirt no more than does the lady
with her vacuum cleaners. Garbage can be handled without human contact. It is only a question of time till
coal-mining will be abandoned in favor of subterranean
extraction and distillation by machinery. In short,

the amount of disagreeable work remaining to be done will be inconsequential. Indeed the past disagreeableness of certain tasks has been chiefly a matter of conditions and stigma which will have no place in a sane society.

It goes without saying that the new economic order will be on a world basis, not obstructed by tariffs and other inefficiencies of shortsighted particularism. As Benjamin Franklin is reputed to have remarked on one occasion, "We must all hang together or we shall all hang separately." How difficult will be the problem of getting acceptance for our "one world" is evidenced by the revival of nuisance tariffs between American states after we thought that the United States had demonstrated the merits of a continental economy. If we do not care enough to have the Supreme Court wipe out such anachronisms, when shall we decide to outlaw barriers on international trade? Such a step is, however, essential to a balanced world economy.

In short, an adequate economic system will pool all world resources and all human labor in behalf of the emancipation of mankind from scarcity and insecurity, and there can be no doubt that the planet is rich enough to deliver a better and better life to as large a population as we shall care to produce if only effort is co-ordinated, science encouraged, and waste eliminated. The task cannot, however, be left to politicians and governments of political states. An economic administration of things is something vastly different from domination over persons, and we shall need to develop new agencies of regional and over-all control which will prove themselves not by cleverness in manipulation or by skill in diplomacy but by forthright competence on the economic level.

It may thus turn out that the interest of the populace in common concerns can be recaptured, revivified, and enlightened to the point where economic efficiency will constitute the nucleus of socialization and of personal culture.

24

SOCIAL REGENERATION

BECAUSE the structure of our social order is so much worse than is the general disposition of the individual, the immediate human problem is not so much how to regenerate more people, or even how to better the conduct of right-hearted individuals, as it is how to apply intelligence so as to make the pattern of society as good as is the disposition of the ordinary person, who "means well" though he may be far from carrying his better impulses into consistent action. That is to say, the plan of our society could be vastly improved without presuming a preliminary improvement of "human nature" and without putting any impossible strain on human nature as it is.

Man's chief sin, indeed, has not been malice but carelessness. Individuals and groups have pursued their own interests with little regard to the over-all consequences of their behavior, and thus have inadvertently inflicted damage that they could have avoided. Moreover, as a byproduct of such negligence we have developed a social order such as no intelligent and reasonably well-meaning person would have conceived of if he had directed his thoughts toward the making of a livable pattern for human society. By default rather than by viciousness we have suffered planlessness and waste to become engrained until now they seem normal and it is hard to make their fatuity seem reprehensible. More-over as suppositious beneficiaries of the present confusion we find ourselves averse to trying for something better.

If it be asked, then, whether the prime obstacle to a better world is stupidity or meanness, it may be said that the two faults certainly reinforce one another. Our selfishness clings to the supposed benefits of an outmoded order, and our blindness keeps us from seeing that the benefits are mostly illusory or self-destroying, just as individualism erases individuality. The large immediate hope for improvement rests, however, in the increase of practical intelligence, which would release many constructive and socially helpful impulses and bridle many of the stupidly self-regarding tendencies. It might, in short, be possible to convince man that there is no such thing as beating the game. If only man could come to believe that it is safe to give free play to his "better nature," the general world problem would be open for solution.

The first effort must be to give progressive thought the upper hand in the channels of publicity, propaganda, and education. If people were sufficiently well informed, they would react much more wholesomely than they are doing. They might even come to behave as well as human nature would permit instead of suffering their public interests to operate at a level so far below that of normal individual behavior. Very few persons, for example, would deliberately inflict on a pestiferous neighbor anything comparable to the devastation carried in the atomic bomb, but such devices are entirely in accord with the pattern that most of the best of mankind take for granted as appropriate to our collective life.

Inasmuch, however, as the conventional and the thoughtless dominate the world's consciousness, such as are willing to think harder and deeper than the rule will have to exert themselves to the limit, and sacrifice to the extreme to create new channels of thought and interest that will be capable of bringing the masses up to the level where they will support a social program as good as man's nature permits instead of continuing on a basis scarcely good enough to offer much hope of survival. If existing schools, churches, newspapers, and radio networks are too much in bondage to inertia, too complaisant in the face of impending ruin, then it becomes necessary to establish new lines of communication and to make them effective.

Existing social patterns, that is, are too disingenuous, too incoherent, too much in bondage to privilege to offer an acceptable basis for saving the world. People in general are capable of understanding, approving, accepting, and operating much better schemes of organization and function than any that now govern nations or have been seriously proposed for the world. Moreover there are enough people competent to prepare and put over essential reorganization if only they would stand together and support one another instead of suffering themselves to be picked off one by one and ruined by the forces of inertia and reaction. Individual heroism is not an adequate answer to the world's dilemma.

We need a revolution, a psychological revolution

comparable in sweep to what we call the Industrial Revolution, which mechanized the thought and feeling and action of the world. If people would use a tenth of their intellectual potential and accelerate their mental processes to a tempo commensurate with modern life, it would be possible to put the world and mankind on an assured basis. Perhaps socialized psychoanalysis applied to society at large might turn the trick, or maybe the semanticists are equal to the occasion, but surely a master effort at redirection of the social spirit, something that far transcends individual regeneration, falls within the sphere of organized Christianity, which will first have to recognize that the gospel offer is directly addressed to societies and institutions, to nations and to the world. We have, indeed, well-nigh forgotten the vision of the Holy City and the promise that "the nations of those being saved will walk in the light of it.'

In an unregenerate society, such as the present, it is supremely hard for most people to be as good as they would aspire to be, and those that try hardest invite neurosis and collapse. The problem is to erect a social pattern that will support, reinforce, and energize people's better natures instead of undermining and thwarting them as do the prevailing patterns of today. Certainly a way of life arrived at inadvertently and by chance, such as ours is, is an anachronism in a world of science, where intelligence is supposed to be doing its perfect work. Moreover after all the brainpower needed has been applied to Nature, there will be an abundant residue for men of good will to consecrate to the redemption of

146

society. There is, indeed, more than enough within Christian circles, if only it were released and focused on the major task of actually and concretely saving the world instead of trying merely to save a few souls out of the hastening wreck.

The salvation of souls is always, indeed, incidental to the building of the Kingdom of God, and undue concentration on souls caters to and enhances a type of selfishness that defeats the larger purposes of the evangel. True evangelism rallies and marshals men for the establishment of Christ's authority over all things everywhere, and it is within such a dynamic pattern that salvation comes to the participating individuals. Only as social institutions fall in line with the challenge of Christ is a proper climate provided for the evangelization of souls and for their growth in grace. The gospel is indeed the "Gospel of the Kingdom," which signifies the regeneration of the social order.

The world has now reached the stage for a spiritual revolution vaster and deeper than that of Protestantism, which, after all, concerned itself mostly with the fortunes of the "middle class"— the rising business interests. As the fighting wedge, Puritanism gave a morale to capitalism, inculcating industry, thrift, self-denial, and, in general, such virtues as built the modern capitalist world. It seems unlikely, however, that the older Protestant churches can rise to the new occasion of the present, simply because they have been so bound to an epoch that they do not comprehend the new era. As yet there has not arisen within ostensibly Christian circles any coherent group of sufficient promise to encourage the hope that the church as we have known it can rise to the task of ushering in the "world to come of which we speak." On the other hand, communism has aborted into Stalinism, which offers nothing to the higher nature of man. Thus in both secular and sacred terms humanity is deadlocked, and the whole creation is groaning in pain "waiting for the manifestation of the children of God."

Some, of course, contend that the world has become so matter-of-fact, so prosaic, so literal, so secular, that the new reformation will be couched in purely worldly terms as befits a scientific age! There is such a thing, however, as being so scientific that one becomes unscientific, as would be the case if one considered man as an impersonal calculating machine. So far indeed is man from being rational that we cannot tell whether he is rational enough to take the simple steps that would avoid ruin. We still live in a world of figurative, symbolic, poetic, emotional experience, which overshadows our sheer rationality. Not being able to get man to use effectively what modicum of reason and logic he might wield, we fall back inevitably on sentiment, and try to stir men's souls to deeper interests and higher values.

Unfortunately we have so far been satisfied with tenuous ideals and shadowy fancies. Abstract piety has paralyzed what should have been the church militant. Leadership, instead of expecting to arouse mass initiative from below, is mainly satisfied to inject an emotional current from above, whereby the masses of the world are entrapped in their loyalties and made subservient to the schemes of sordid political leadership. Nowhere in the world does organized Christianity venture to offer a plausible alternative to pagan statecraft. Pious resolutions are, to be sure, passed in great numbers, but the church is not calling its people away from the next war. The challenge to social regeneration is scarcely formulated let alone offered with any ringing insistence. To implement the gospel of the kingdom is the Christian imperative for our day.

25

PERSONAL INTEGRATION

WHEN the Christian evangel is presented as "the gospel of the Kingdom," reassurance comes to the individual in the realization that only through Christianization of the social order are right conditions afforded for the highest spiritual development and growth in grace. Indeed it is apparent that the validity of the Kingdom is to be measured by its effect on personality, which offers the only measure of whether anything is worth while.

Meanwhile, however, the Christian must wrestle with the unwieldy circumstances of an unruly world, and must wrest from an uncongenial environment whatever possibilities he can find for the growth and refinement of personality. Indeed the upshot of our investigation is to bring home to the individual the imperatives of Christianity as the vehicle of integration, personal as well as social.

Integration as the goal of all human development consists, then, in internal balance and external adjustment, a standard as applicable to the individual as it is to societies or to mankind as a collective whole, for no personality shows integration save as it manifests internal equilibrium, which is possible only when there is a right relation with the whole scheme of life. Only the duly socialized personality gives evidence of regeneration and redemption.

PERSONAL INTEGRATION

Whatever, then, is done in the way of soul culture consists essentially in the attainment of organic wholeness of experience, which cannot be accomplished as long as the person is in bondage to mechanistic patterns of thinking, which in spite of their seeming precision are always piecemeal and essentially incoherent, so that they are irreconcilable with integrity of feeling and action.

Most people, therefore, will have to re-educate themselves or accept re-education before they can approach the fullness of the Christian life, which is not a matter of blue-prints, habit formation, character building, but of effective reorientation toward an inclusive and absorbing goal. Such re-education will bring home to the learner that patchwork changes never accomplish essential improvement in either personality or society, as Jesus so forcibly indicated by his illustration of the patch and the garment. Only as the individual or the society becomes willing to experience regeneration is there any hope for escape from the besetting ills that afflict a pagan culture.

Because, moreover, the mechanistic pattern of thought and action have been so deeply engrained by our common experience in an imposingly mechanized world, the task of eradicating the perverse bias and retrieving organic wholeness in personal and social life must be painstakingly tedious for the average man. One reading of this book, with all its iterations and reiterations, even though acceptance follow, will be no more than a beginning. So much has to be unlearned that it will be more than a lifetime before the soul has completely recovered from the materialistic, mechanistic distortion inflicted by a dehumanized culture. The present effort in educational circles for the recovery of the "liberal arts" ideal through "general education" is but a feeble and shadowy beginning on a cultural task that will require the energies of generations for its accomplishment. Meanwhile responsible individuals will do their utmost to make sure that they learn nothing piecemeal, but that everything they attain is rooted and clarified through a realization of its integral relation to all other facts and interests as inextricable aspects of an organic wholeness of universal experience. Everyone, that is, must aspire to be a philosopher, for Christianity teaches that all things hold together and work together, so that duty and aspiration are not multifarious but integral. The Kingdom of God is indeed a totalitarian society.

In proportion, then, as the individual becomes organismic in his thinking he will recover a sense of the wholeness of life, and when he faces the labyrinth thrust upon him by modern society he will not look for advance through petty, unrelated, piecemeal, and incoherent reforms, but will accept only such proposals as are in their essence imperative steps toward the integral triumph of a Christian social order. He will be immune to the social quackery that would suppress symptoms, and will address himself to the constitutional malady that vitiates a pagan society bent on subordinating people to things and on accomplishing the complete stultification of life and negation of personality through diabolical technics.

As a member of a church, the sole duty of which is

to accomplish the triumph of the Kingdom of God, he will judge church programs and functions by the integral standard, and will not be impressed by mere busy work, or by hectic activities designed only to divert the saints or to comfort the camp-followers. The pastor will be primarily a prophet leading the advance guard, and will not suffer himself to be diverted by the interest of parishoners in self-indulgence, even though the dissipation sought be ostensibly spiritual.

When the Christian contemplates his relation to the environing community, he will not focus on odds and ends, but at every point will ask precisely what needs to be done in order to accomplish another step toward the ascendancy of Christ in the pattern as well as in the conduct of community life. Vices will loom less large in his appraisal than will those perfectly respectable and orderly arrangements whereby neighbor gets the better of neighbor and whereby irresponsible persons attain a position of control over the lives of others.

In the realm of citizenship the integral personality will repudiate the specious standards of allegedly practical politics, which are always unprincipled and short-sighted, and will address himself to asserting the claims of ultimate principles upon the allegiance of citizens. He will not hesitate to "throw away his vote" when integrity so requires, and will sometimes take comfort in the old saw that "it is better to vote for what you want and not get it than to vote for what you don't want and get it."

In all these realms of life, the Christian will be concerned less with mere personal rectitude, in the sense of "keeping his own skirts clean," than he will with effective organization for positive righteousness. Likewise he will not be overconcerned about the fortunes of any group smaller than the human race, but will come to view the welfare of family, neighborhood, state, and nation as a function of the welfare of mankind. As the educational director of a Farmers' Union region remarked in rebuttal of a current jibe, "Unless we are prepared to guarantee a quart of milk to every Hottentot, we cannot guarantee a quart to every child in Kansas." Obviously no spot has any economic security save in terms of a world market; and no society, however local and substantial, has any guarantees such as flow from the soundness of the world order.

The Christian is assured thus that there is no room for any attempt at special privilege for any individual or any social group. Indeed attempt at special privilege is a confession of inferiority, evidenced by fear of inability to hold one's own in a fair race or of incapacity for finding contentment in the circumstances that can be shared by all mankind. Walt Whitman was fundamentally sound and Christian in his refusal to accept for himself anything that could not be had by any other person on the same terms.

In what, then, consists that personal salvation on which Protestantism has so largely concentrated? Certainly we have no right to belittle Christianity into a selfish scheme for personal insurance, or to feature the priestly office of Christ at the expense of his claims as teacher and lord; but few are so magnanimous as not to be concerned about what may come to them in consequence of a demanding life program. What is "the salvation purchased by Christ"?

The essence of salvation in the Christian sense is that one is kept from going to waste. The very slight attention given to the future life by the writers of scripture almost forbids the strenuous attempts often made to build a picture of heaven and its joys out of scattering hints. It is as if we were debarred from imagining eternity just as we are debarred from making mental pictures of God. The Christian emphasis is not on what one may get by becoming a Christian, but on what one may give and achieve. Thus the appeal is to everyone that wants to amount to something, to count for something, and salvation is not primarily avoidance of penalty but equipment for success. "Seekest thou great things for thyself? Seek them not!"

The upshot of the whole matter is that in the crisis of the present age everything hinges on whether man can learn to think, and feel, and act organismically rather than mechanistically, whether he can learn to deal in organic wholes rather than in incoherent parts, whether he can learn to be integral rather than remain at cross-purposes. On all these points Christian thought holds to the assurance that God is the wholeness of experience, that Christ is the meaning of the universe, and that in Him all things hold together and work together in the interest of those that respond to His purpose, "till we all come in the unity of the faith and the knowledge of the son of God, to a perfect man, to the measure of the stature of the fulness of Christ" in "the Holy City, the new Jerusalem, coming down out of heaven from God."

155